FRESH
PAINT

Stephen Lynch

Printed in the United States of America

First Printing, 2020

ISBN 978-0-578-76893-9

Fresh Paint Innovative Products LLC

539 W. Commerce St. Suite #2975

Dallas, TX 75208

www.soulministry.com

Fresh Paint Dedicated to My Wife Mary Lynch

Table of Contents

Introduction

This book includes true life experiences from 20 years of pastoral counseling and 40 years of marriage. My marriage after all these years still exhibits the same passion and heartfelt love which bonds our relationship. My objective is to share insight into solutions that assisted many individuals to overcome marital and family issues. In addition, I have included actual sessions of real-life situations. It is difficult to understand why love is simply not perfect. During the search to find true love, we allow another person access to an emotional, sacred place. The desire to find true love and build a lasting relationship can often result in a traumatic emotional experience. True love is wonderful, but it exhibits growing pains as a relationship develops. How could something so pure and with a deep emotional connection go so terribly wrong. These life experiences create an emotional layer like a painted object with several layers of paint. Every person has multiple emotional layers which represent the outcome of each relationship. Each layer is like a paint with different colors which represent a significant life occurrence. These different layers shape your personality. It is often a valiant effort to disguise this pain among friends, which is hidden behind a gentle smile. New partners' emotional state of mind is guided by experiences of previous relationships. These layers are carried into new relationships and fresh pain can be brought back to life by exposure to similar circumstances of abuse. Once the emotional pains are reactivated, it will refresh the memory of the previous experience and the pain restarts. All life's experiences consist of different emotional layers which shape our overall perspective. To understand and relate to a new partner, you must be in control of your emotional state of mind. In addition, understand that they have emotional layers as well. It would be easy to understand a person's reaction if you were aware of their past experiences.

Fresh Paint addresses the emotional rollercoaster and how to overcome these experiences. I will share suggestions on how to come out of these dark places and help others endure similar circumstances. During my pastoral tenure, I provided marital counseling and relationship coaching to assist couples to overcome these difficult experiences. It is important to learn how to overcome past relationships and remain in a healthy emotional place. I will offer guidance for maneuvering through relationships from dating to problem-solving and restoration of the sizzle in a relationship.

Fresh Paint will address common questions and issues regarding relationships and specific family matters crisis.

Relationship Issues

Why many of my relationships crash and burn?

How do I know my mate really loves me?

Life after divorce

How to resolve conflicts

Toxic relationships

Learning to love again

Reason partner's cheat

Family Crisis Matters

How a family deals with terminal illness

Coping with the loss of a loved one

Caregivers

Caring for the differently abled

Suicide—The Pain left behind

Bullying

Parental abandonment

This book provides practical instructions regarding how a person can overcome emotional experiences and how to coach a person through these life-changing events. The will and resilience of the human spirit along with faith can overcome the condemnation, depression, and the feeling that no one understands you. We are created to be victorious, but it requires overcoming the devastating and traumatic events of trials and tribulations.

Chapter: 1 First Love

We often reflect and use the term "first love." It usually happens during adolescence as our emotions evolve toward maturity. Our heart desires companionship and someone to love. These emotions are driven by peer pressure and natural attraction between a man and a woman. We must understand these natural instincts were made and instilled within us when we were created. During our youth, life was full of fantasies, thoughts of romance, and the desire to share these feelings with a partner. I can remember the crush that existed with young girls during the school days who were thrilled to be wearing their boyfriend's football jacket. These courtship times lead to the first emotional development in most relationships. As you know many of these relationships have a short life and end, many times, abruptly. Many of us remember the sorrow and heartbreak from our youth and the pain associated with the end of a relationship. These experiences began to mold our personality and how we handle new relationships. Our first love sometimes was reckless and giddy and created a feeling never experienced before.

Young adult's physically develop faster than they do mentally or spiritually. Many are not ready for the consequences associated with true love. These failed relationships began to build an emotional layer in their mind, which builds a template for future relationships. It is often said do not play with another person's emotions. Because emotions are many times in the driver's seat, they sometimes make a fool out of us. This period of development requires proper guidance from peers to ensure they are well informed regarding the pitfalls of relationships. It is common for the youth to reject guidance and feel parents are overprotective. The youth have a sense of maturity but lack the emotional skills to manage their relationships without parental oversight.

First Love Story

I remember in high school one student in the school band fell madly in love. She was his first girlfriend. He was a loner and was not aggressive in pursuing relationships. He was the average-looking, happy-go-lucky guy who was unpopular, but was athletic. The young lady had similar attributes, so they were a perfect match. They were ecstatic because they had found true love. Every day they would sit together full of puppy love. They were practically inseparable. One day the news spread that the guy was in the cafeteria and crying in despair. His true love had met an older student from another high school and had dissolved their relationship. Everyone felt so sorry for him and felt his pain. He had to deal with the embarrassment and the ridicule from other students. In addition, no one could calm his pain. He continued to plead with her to reconcile their relationship, to no avail. This incident led to the development of his first ever emotional pain. He slowly recovered over the next several weeks and would cry every time he passed by her in the hallway. She however expressed no remorse and had moved on. He received support from his friends and adjusted to his heartbreak and returned to his jovial personality.

Sexual Desires

It is often the parents who ignore their young adult children's desires to explore their sexuality. Some parents believe their child is different and is not sexually active. Due to this assumption, many times, the parents are the last one to know about their activities. Parents have the responsibility to maintain open lines of communication, so no subject is off the table. The word "sex" is often of great taboo in the home. Therefore, it is randomly discussed so many young adults acquire knowledge from peers. Peers will provide instructions which could prove detrimental to these young adults safety and emotional well-being. It is the parents who assume all the responsibility of their young adults regardless of the outcome, whether it is teenage pregnancy or sexually transmitted diseases. Parents must develop a climate for open dialogue, so that these children are comfortable to discuss these sensitive matters with the parents. Parents have real-life experiences they can share with their children. One of the greatest tricks young men use is to pretend to be the perfect boyfriend in order to draw a young woman into a relationship, giving the appearance of a perfect love affair. Then they pressurize for intimacy as proof of their love or threaten to terminate the relationship. Such pressure on a young woman who is without proper guidance can fall victim to teen pregnancy. The exposure to embarrassment when their suitor spreads the news to their peers or terminates the relationship after intimacy is an added pressure. It is possible for either member of the sex to fall prey to such pressures.

Lovesickness

When a loving relationship full of bliss and emotional fulfillment turns sour, it leaves a sense of emptiness and despair. It is during these times that a person experiences an emotional condition called "lovesickness." Some may bounce back in a short period of time, but some may face difficulty in overcoming this fresh pain. They may develop mood swings and a void feeling on the inside. Some may resolve the problem with their mate and reconcile their conflict. If this does not occur, they must cope with the termination of their relationship. This experience creates an emotional layer like paint that is covered up but remains in individuals' memories throughout their life. These emotional experiences help them prepare their emotions for the next relationship. A lovesick person may exhibit the following symptoms: loss of appetite, binge eating, self-isolation, emotional outbursts, crying bouts, and lack of hygiene. A lovesick person can be driven to a dark place, but the good news is they can overcome this experience. Do not allow depression to keep you in a dark place. You were wonderfully created and designed to overcome this pain. It is easy to blame someone or yourself. No matter the cause of the cessation of the relationship, if it cannot be reconciled, it is time to release yourself emotionally.

It also can take a person into isolation, causing them to withdraw from their friends and relatives. Heartbreak is just like a cut; first it must heal and afterwards leave a scar. These individuals suffer real mental anguish, and just like a scar, it remains in their memory for a lifetime. If you have ever experienced heartbreak, you can identify with the emotional turmoil when you loved so deeply but it was not reciprocated. No one enjoys the pain of being rejected by someone you love.

To help a friend process, heal, and move forward, it requires an understanding of their emotional state. Most people experience several relationships but only a few enter the place where a person has accessed their innermost being. This emotional place is reserved for only those you genuinely love. When this bond has been severed, it creates a vacuum of depression until the heart heals from the fresh pain. It is important to allow a true friend to provide moral support and good, sound advice during testing times. The first step is to support this person without condemning their decisions or demeaning their mate and reassuring them with your unbiased support. Those who provide advice during this time must remember if the couple reconciles, they will remember all your positive, or negative, comments regarding their mate. It is important to empathize and not enable this person, so they embrace the recovery and focus on the positive. Focusing on the positive includes helping them emotionally and being patient just a good friend who will support them through this situation. The goal is to ensure they are in a healthy place emotionally. It is good to spend private time alone with them or participate in recreational outings. What they experienced was real therefore do not exacerbate the situation with critical comments.

Dating

Can you remember your first date? During the teenage years there was a process to the first date. The old-school parental way back in the day required the parents to meet the young men who desired to date their daughter. They would allow regular home visits to evaluate his background and conduct family discussions with their family. The prospective young man was allowed to only sit beside their daughter during his visit. During this time, the parents would review your family tree to check the suitor's background. This process continued until the family was comfortable with your presence. It was not allowable to hold hands or even have an occasional embrace or even think about a kiss. Once you passed the family review, it was permissible to have your first movie date. This was exciting because after being under examination for weeks, now it was a time to spend some quality time alone and maybe get one kiss. The first date was exciting, and your imagination would just run wild. The time for the first date had finally arrived and you were well-groomed, drenched in the best cologne available. You have definitely arrived early to pick up your date. Your date steps out with a beautiful smile, and you being the perfect gentleman, would open the car door. Just out of nowhere, someone jumps into the backseat and inquires where you are going. It was to my surprise we had a chaperone on our first date. This person's sole responsibility was to ensure all our activities were honorable. I know this sounds archaic compared to modern-day dating, but regardless everyone remembers their first date.

Dating is the beginning of a relationship when it has evolved from being more than a friendship. It is a chance to compare values, commonalities, and interests. It creates a playing field to explore the feelings created from the initial attraction. It is also important to know each person has values and experiences from prior affairs that may affect their tolerance levels in this new relationship. Our emotions are developed from real-life experiences, whether they are good or bad. Sometimes when a person has experienced harm in a prior relationship, they will move too quickly by entering in another before they have overcome the pain from the previous experience. One of the greatest mistakes in a relationship is to build it upon intimacy rather than allowing the relationship to evolve from friendship. These relationships often crash and burn due to lack of substance. Never let your body be the main attraction in a relationship because the flame will soon fade. It is important to not feel desperate actions are necessary to satisfy your partner. Each partner must appreciate individual personal qualities and allow the relationship to grow. We were created to love and respect each other. How a partner treats you on a date is a preview of what is to come. Another great mistake is the idea that you have the power to change a person. You are just at the point of love at first site, but this person has some habits and existing behaviors, which must be notated. The power to change can be influenced by a caring person but that person must have the desire to change. The great attributes exhibited during a date should be respect, a good listener, patient, and considerate of your interest.

Dating with Self-Confidence

It is important to have self-confidence while dating. This mind-set is to set mental parameters to understand that dating is exploratory and will allow better insight regarding their personality. While dating it requires you to focus on the things that matter regardless of their appearance, popularity, and financial status. It is a recipe for failure if you do not use good judgment to influence your decisions to build a good relationship. This really means you should not lower personal standards or compromise your integrity for the sake of love. Dating with confidence simply requires you to respect yourself and allow your partner to see your true attributes. During the dating period, you are not "stuck up" but are a person who exhibits a level of respect which is required to build a close friendship. One of the greatest fears is being alone. Most couples desire to have someone to spend time with at recreational activities. In addition they desire to be attractive to the opposite sex. It is these factors which cause many to stay in a relationship and really know this person is not the right one. There is nothing wrong with a friendly relationship, but often, one partner desires more than the other. It is better to be open about your intentions which are based on building a friendship. This will establish from the beginning your intentions and keep your partner aware where they stand in the relationship. Dating with confidence allows you to be comfortable with pretense or a strong desire to be someone you are not. A person who finds you attractive will eventually evaluate your personality more than other characteristics. Your relationship will develop and grow because of the wonderful person you exhibit in their presence.

How Do I Know My Mate Really Loves Me?

One intriguing question during the development of a relationship which seems to be almost perfect is. "Does my mate really love me?" Love is more than a strong affection, but it is the details that tell the story. Love first starts with trust and the desire to be honest and open during a relationship.

In addition, love includes faithfulness with a genuine concern exhibited by a person's action, willingness to compromise, and being a good listener. Many say it was love at first sight! A relationship may seem wonderful until the first serious disagreement occurs, and the strength of a relationship will be measured by the ability of two people to reconcile their differences. Love defined by many women is:" How does this person who loves me react when we both disagree?" This will require them to compromise to facilitate a solution. They should display characteristics which show genuine concern such as an apology when wrong, right temperament, and willingness to compromise. Of course, in a perfect world these are the correct answers, but it will take work to develop these traits. True love however will stand the test.

One of the misconceptions when disagreements occur is to buy things to appease your partner rather than discussing the problem. A person who loves you should display respect even when they are frustrated. Abusive language and physical attacks are a sure sign a relationship may develop serious issues. It is important to resolve these issues before they escalate any further. No one should feel this type of conduct is acceptable and communicate to their mate what behaviors are unacceptable.

I met a couple who had been married over 40 years to conduct a survey of how they remained together for all these years. One of the main responses was to never lose your excitement and friendship which brought them together. In addition, be willing to forgive each other when disagreements occur. It was important to spend quality time with each other and never let the relationship lose its importance. Marriage is a special bond and does not just happen; it requires work, patience, support and a willingness to compromise.

One-in-a-Million Mentality

A person who loves you should demonstrate by their conduct that you are one in a million-special person. This will be demonstrated by their actions when they spend quality time with you to build a long-term relationship. To build a strong relationship, it starts with a commitment between two individuals who have developed a bond of trust. This trust builds continually based upon each other's respect and treatment during the relationship. Trust is not based upon poetic phrases and expensive gifts but mutual respect. It is not just an ordinary relationship or friends with benefits but has substance beyond intimacy

It may sound mushy, but it has a level of excitement when two people have a relationship based upon trust and compatibility. This one-in-a-million mentality is acknowledging the divine creativity of God when he made this person unique and one of a kind. It includes loving them without being in control or dictating their lives, but allowing them to be who they are and enjoying their presence. Many times it is the big ego and the unwillingness to say the two words that have more power than any act of reconciliation. These two words are "I apologize." The expression of an apology backed by a genuine commitment to not continue a certain behavior can solve a lot of disagreements. Couples who can be honest with their emotions and recognize when they are wrong can build a long-lasting relationship.

Love is obvious

True love is obvious and requires no excuses for consistent bad behavior or lack of respect. Love has growing pains which requires learning how to resolve conflicts in a reasonable way. If a person genuinely loves you, they will not give up and will demonstrate the appropriate behavior to show remorse. Love is obvious, and it includes how people act when they are happy or angry. It is difficult to understand why a person who loves another person would mentally and physically abuse them. They must take the proper action to rectify this behavior. There are many factors that cause behavioral issues to come to the surface, but they must be addressed, or things will remain the same.

Love is obvious if something is offensive and toxic to a relationship it is important to explore all solutions such as professional counselling. It is a smart decision to seek professional help if necessary because an objective opinion can explain both perspectives. Many times, the obvious love is overlooked by the person close to you because they are considered a safe relationship. A safe relationship is a friendship that has not fully evolved to a serious partnership.

To demonstrate true love, a person must really understand what it means. Love is just not based on your emotional feelings for your partner. True love is mutual, and both partners have made a commitment, with a foundation built on trust. Love is really the ultimate definition of trust. It must be mutual because too many times it is one-sided, whereby one partner does not have the same level of commitment. Lasting relationships are slowly built with tender, loving care and with open communication. The best way to demonstrate true love is how you treat your partner. A relationship in which both partners can share their innermost feelings is the beginning of something special.

This is a very sensitive matter because it involves how your partner was raised and who has a major influence in their lives. During the relationship-building process, some relationships crash and burn allowing battle lines to be drawn before the relationship can grow.

It is the Little Things That Count the Most

How do I know my mate really loves me? It is the little things that matter the most. Sometimes in a relationship, many place emphasis on the big things, but it is the little things which have the most value. Little things such as being a good listener, affectionate, considerate of your mate's desires, and spontaneous adaptability to recreational activities. The reality of little things has true value and are a better indicator of how a person cares emotionally. A good relationship is built upon friendship, compatibility, and respect. Sometimes our focus is on the bigger things, especially gifts.

Try the five-dollar investment of purchasing five "I'm thinking of you" cards and mail them daily to your mate's workplace or home. Each day they have a gentle reminder of your love. How you treat me is one of those little things that matter the most. Your kindness and warm smile have a far greater value than silver or gold.

Recognizing the positive things your soul mate does will foster an atmosphere for love to flourish. Spend quality time holding hands, sharing memories, and appreciating that delicious meal. Share compliments! Send a simple card or text message to say I love you. It is the little things from the heart which reflect your innermost affection for those you love. Love must be shared daily in the simplest forms. It is often made complicated by drama, but true love is simply good manners. Treating each other with dignity and respect. Real lovers read each other's emotional mode and can know by your temperament if you are having a bad day or just need a hug. They do not judge each other but offer encouragement and genuine concern. They are a sounding board for your concerns, no matter how small; if it bothers you, it is important to them. The little things are spontaneous, simply because they care. You cannot buy love; it does not have a price.

True love must be earned and is obvious. The greatest gift in the Bible is love. It is not intended to be hidden in the heart without emotions but to be exhibited daily. Sending flowers to show love is a great idea, but if you did something wrong, accept responsibility and apologize. Your actions speak louder than any gift.

Chapter 2: Why Many Relationships Crash and Burn

Physical Attraction

How can a relationship between two people that starts off sizzling hot end so abruptly and without a well-defined reason?

The sizzle in the relationship is probably founded on physical attraction. Physical attraction can be defined as the level in which an individual's physical features are attractive to another individual. According to research, people will often choose someone they find physically attractive for a romantic partner (Little, Jones, & DeBruine, 2011). After all, it can be difficult to measure any other personal characteristic such as sense of humor, personality, honesty, or intelligence when meeting an individual for the first time.

The attraction between a man and woman was designed from the beginning of our creation (Halberstadt, 2006). When God said it was not good for man to be alone, God designed a woman to fulfill the needs of the man. While a man was designed to fulfill a woman's needs. This initial physical attraction would always exist between a man and a woman. Initial attraction is based on outward appearance such as shape, height, voice, eyes, walk, or mannerism.

How important is physical attraction in a romantic relationship?

Physical attraction is shown to be one of the important factors in the beginning of a relationship (Jones et al., 2011). However, relationships based on simply physical attraction may not have time to build a foundation that is generally required for a lasting connection. A common pitfall of romance founded on physical attraction or a sexy setting is the struggle to survive because of a lack of substance.

I conducted a survey among young couples to discover their major concerns regarding romantic relationships. A top area of concern according to the surveyed couples was compatibility. Another key area of concern according to the surveyed couples was long-term aspirations. Physical attraction or outward appearance was not a top concern.

Common Interest

A common misconception is that opposites attract, but true, lasting relationships will have difficulty surviving when the individuals are not compatible.

So, what is compatibility? Compatibility can be defined simply as two people sharing common interests. Common interest includes similar desires regarding recreational and day-to-day activities. In addition, common interests may include hobbies designed around participating in group activities. Individuals who are not compatible have interest that are unlike the interests of their partner. This is not to say that all couples must have the same common interest, but when interests are totally conflicting, additional pressure will be placed on a relationship. In most cases, non-compatibility causes many relationships to dissolve before a real foundation can be established.

Relationships are generally stronger when partners enjoy similar activities. Similar activities can be described as having shared desires, behaviors, or actions relating to enjoyment, recreation, pleasure, or viewpoint. When we have a lot in common with another person, this could mean we like or enjoy doing similar things or hobbies such as going to the movies or eating at a certain type of restaurant. This could also include having a similar religion, social view, or habit. For example, two people having similar social views may enjoy going to a conference or event relating to a common topic like animal cruelty.

In some instances, one partner may not have experienced an activity, but in the new relationship, the partner may become exposed to something new. These new ventures they may learn to enjoy. Exploring new interests when building a new relationship can be fun. However, if the new activity is disliked or unbearable, the partner exploring the new activity must provide honest feedback.

What are long-term aspirations? It is also important for partners to understand each other's long-term aspirations or goals. Long-term aspirations allow one or both partners a look inside how the relationship is viewed by their partner. For example, a common relationship aspiration is to get married, have children, or to one day buy a house with a white picket fence. Knowing your partner's long-term goal can ensure you are aware of their values. In addition, this provides a vision for their future lifestyle. For example, it makes no sense to plan a long-term future with someone who clearly does not want a long-term relationship. Another example would be to plan on raising a family with an individual who has no desire to have children.

Relationships that last are usually built on a foundation of friendship and trust (Grover & Helliwell, 2019). However, compatibility and knowing your partner's long-term aspirations are also shown to be essential elements in successful relationships.

Other Key Components in Successful Relationships

I conducted a survey among several single individuals to find out the qualities they find most important in a relationship. Their responses were:

o   vision and a plan;

o   financial stability; and

o   maturity level.

Vision and a Plan

It is surprising most women do not mention physical attraction as being an essential attribute when looking for a partner. However, for men physical attraction is sometimes the initial motivation, but not the main one. A common quality that both men and women look for in a potential long-term relationship is vision.

What does it mean to have a vision?

Although relationships are truly built on friendship, it is equally important to know what your partner's vision is for the present and the future. Their vision provides a view into their thought process, because for their vision to occur, they must have a plan. Their plan must include details and the analytics on how to transform their vision into reality. Without vision, a relationship can become stagnant and less desirable for individuals seeking a long-term partner.

It is also important for the person seeking a true relationship to evaluate the intelligence of a potential partner. This can be accomplished by knowing if the individual has developed a plan for their life. A person without a vision does not have a plan. A plan allows a potential partner to understand how or if they will fit into a partner's future. Many times, individuals who are compatible during discussion reveal they have a similar vision and plan.

It is possible to have a successful relationship without a vision and a plan, but those seeking a serious relationship, may require one to establish a level of security.

Financial Stability

A major concern for individuals contemplating a serious relationship or marriage is the financial resources a partner will bring to the union. Love is a wonderful thing but unfortunately bills must still be paid. A relationship can be filled with love, but some individuals may be reluctant to continue the relationship or go to the next level because of financial reasons.

Financial stability allows each partner comfort in knowing that a continued relationship will include a certain type of lifestyle. A lifestyle which includes financial resources to pay for basic necessities, and then some. This is a natural concern for most individuals searching for a suitable partner.

This does not mean that an individual seeking a more stable partner is a "gold digger," but it does allow them to feel more secure if the potential mate is financially stable. In addition, many common problems in relationships exist because of financial issues. Financial instability can result in a tremendous amount of unwanted pressure and stress on a relationship. I am not saying an individual must be financially stable to be a good partner, but most people prefer individuals having more financial resources. Then again, financial stability can still be obtained if two people who are in love develop a plan to improve financial capabilities while in the dating stages of a relationship.

Maturity level

Maturity level is also shown to be an important aspect in long-term relationships. If either partner is not emotionally mature, their mind-set can be focused on enjoying the moment rather than developing a lasting romance. A mature individual is typically able to maintain long-term commitments, whereas an individual who is less mature generally has a mind-set geared toward enjoying the moment. Relationships between immature individuals are more explorative, fun-loving, and based on thrill-seeking. Also, the primary goals of these types of relationships are generally fixated on intimacy and gratification, not on long-term commitment. Relationships between immature individuals (one or both partners) can still grow and evolve; however, one or both partners must be willing to wait and allow the relationship to build a more solid foundation.

Relationships Based on Intimacy

Relationships based strictly on intimacy that began with fireworks and sizzle can fizzle out just as fast. Desiring to develop a relationship based on intimacy will not allow friendship and courtship to build the fabric necessary to sustain and hold a lasting connection. Pressure to remain in the relationship may entice a partner to become more intimate, an idea, which at the time may appear logical but lead to just a fun-loving experience. However, relationships can be one-sided, which means one partner may be more invested than the other. Consequently, when conflict arises in one-sided relationships, this can easily escalate to separation.

Remember, relationships must have trust and friendship (Grover & Helliwell, 2019). These attributes allow individuals in a committed relationship a more solid foundation to fall back on during times of conflict.

Intimacy alone does not provide a solid foundation for the relationship to endure conflict (Birnbaum, 2018).

It is surprising how an individual in a relationship based on intimacy will find another person attractive and sexy, but eventually when looking for a long-term partner, the individual's standard can change. Instead of seeking attractiveness and intimacy, new standards may include an individual who is more trustworthy, compassionate, or compatible. More importantly, these new attributes can build a foundation of true love that is more durable.

Relationships based on intimacy can put one partner in a disrespectful situation. Self-respect is an important part of healthy relationships. It is a bad idea to rush into a relationship assuming this may satisfy the needs of a potential partner. Relationships based on intimacy may foster disrespect and lust which eventually cause division. In contrast, more successful relationships are founded on love and respect and are more enduring. In addition, the emotional bond (which is particularly important), along with trust and friendship, can result in a relationship built with substance.

I have counseled or ministered numerous individuals and couples throughout my pastoral and professional career on how to enhance their relationships. In my experience, relationships between individuals who are compatible are usually more successful. Other (more individualistic) components in successful relationships are based on one or both partners having a vision and plan for the relationship, financial stability, and a similar level of maturity.

I have also had the experience of working with couples in relationships that are usually destined to fail. These relationships were often founded on lust or intimacy with no other attributes to fall back on. In addition, unsuccessful relationships often featured individuals who are not compatible, mental and physical abuse, or an unhealthy mixture of personalities. These relationships are one-sided and toxic which can result in numerous difficulties for one or both partners. Furthermore, I discovered that unhealthy unions usually exhibit warning signs in early stages of the relationship. However, some people ignore these warnings and end up in a very unhealthy relationship. These relationships can result in significant consequences for an unwary individual.

Dominant Personalities

This is a very sensitive matter because it involves how your partner was raised and who had a major influence in their life. Many times, your partner may have a dominant person in their life who approves or must validate their relationships. These individuals are people who were role models to shape your partner's future and be their confidants during a crisis. Be careful. Before you start assuming this person is a mother's boy or a person unable to make decisions without their approval, these individuals regardless of relation has assisted your partner with crisis management. I often say we are a product of our environment. During the relationship building process, new relationships can crash and burn due to battle lines being drawn before it can grow. Whenever you enter a serious relationship be aware that your partner's family members may have significant influence on their decisions.

A dominant personality does not always necessarily mean a controlling personality. To understand you must recognize the influence of dominant personalities over your partner so you can be aware of establishing unintended battle lines. Your partner has freewill to make their own decisions, but they may be affected by other important people in their life.

The way to handle a relationship with a dominant personality is to not fall in a trap of a tug of war with your partner. Be open with your mate about your feelings and allow your partner to make an informed decision. If you discover your point of view is consistently being ignored, it will continue long term in your relationship unless you make it known. Taking on a dominant personality directly may lead to confusion and harm your relationship. You have a decision to make regarding how to balance your relationship with a person who has been influenced by a dominant personality.

Remember to establish your tolerance level to ascertain if this will be a problem you can handle. Everyone deserves to be treated with dignity and respect.

Toxic Relationships

Many relationships are described as toxic which means they are not mentally, spiritually, or physically healthy. Good relationships are built upon friendship, compatibility, and mutual respect. Each partner must demonstrate the strength to endure differences of opinion and a willingness to compromise. Great relationships are nurtured with love languages, patience, and trust. Couples should not focus on the past but learn from their mistakes and build a stronger relationship. Toxic relationships start with a sizzle, but as they develop, major problems occur which must be properly addressed.

What is the definition of love?

Love can be described as having strong affection, care, or deep respect for another individual. In many cases some describe love by a strong affection and accept bad behavior based upon these feelings. True love is deeper and more secure. Toxic relationships are those which operate under the cover of a loving, caring relationship, but one partner or both are abusing one another emotionally. The relationships function but are dysfunctional with lack of respect, broken promises and with no long-term commitment to change. These relationships are toxic, full of drama, disputes, infidelity, and mental anguish. A common question is: "Why does one continue to desire a toxic relationship?" A common response to this question, "I am in love and cannot help the way I feel."

Toxic relationships will ultimately end in separation unless action is taken to rectify the problems. These relationships can improve if partners are willing to change. This begins with honesty and expressing to your loved one whose behavior is harmful and not acceptable. If true love exists, then they will listen and accept responsibility for their actions. Partners who refuse to listen and seem in denial of their behavior will eventually destroy their relationship. Any continued abusive behavior during a relationship creates a fresh layer of pain which may impact future relationships.

A common method employed by abusers is to control by manipulation or to make things appear to be sincere and normal. This is designed to destroy a person's self-worth. A physical abuser is the easiest to identify obviously due to the visual evidence of abuse on their mate body. It is difficult to explain when family and friends notice bruises with no clear explanation. The abuser controls their mate by means of fear and blames the victim for their conduct.

Many people ask: Why would a person remain in this situation? Why don't they just leave?

Many times, they are influenced by other factors such as their children or financial dependence. The victim often feels this person genuinely loves them and somehow things will get better. These types of situations require

25

intervention and counseling and can be resolved if the abuser is willing to receive help. Healing for an abuser will only occur when they realize and accept responsibility for their behavior, possibly through counselling.

Seeking professional assistance is not a sign of failure, but of wisdom. Many times, the abuser has issues from their background which created fresh pain that can be defeated with the help of a loved one. The individual may have emotional layers from their past that can impact their present behavior and conduct.

Another type of abuser is an individual with mental control such as a financial advantage which leads to one-sided decision-making. The person impacted by the controller many times feel they do not have a viable option. They feel trapped and often will justify their choice to remain is better than separating from their mate. *It is not my objective to advise anyone to separate from a loved one. My intention is to offer advice on how to find a potential solution for their situation.* I recommend professional assistance from a person with an unbiased opinion. It is up to the individual to establish a tolerance level and decide how to improve the situation from their perspective.

Toxic one-sided relationships are based upon a person assuming they can create a person who will love them by showering them with love, gifts, and intimacy. Due to loneliness and a desire to be in a relationship, some individuals will lower their standards and deny the obvious with the mind-set that they can change another individual. In addition, these individuals are attracted to another person and will try to influence the relationship by purchasing nice gifts. Also, during the early stages of the relationship, they may attempt to buy another person's love by being financially liberal to an individual with limited financial resources, which can create a sense of dependency. As a result, and after financial resources are diminished, the relationship will begin to falter because it was not founded on true love. The expectations were only established on financial needs being met.

No one can buy true love. True love must evolve and develop from a solid foundation of friendship. A one-sided relationship can be based on an individual demanding intimacy in return for their time and attention. In a genuine relationship, a person will love the person who exhibits a valid concern. Individuals who allow themselves to be caught up in relationships based on accepting financial gifts and on one devoid of a true commitment. They may be setting themselves up for failure. A person committed to a relationship will usually demonstrate care in their actions.

Close the Door on Past Relationships

These relationships are like a travelling man who carries old and unwanted luggage to new destinations. Past relationships provide learning and growing experiences. Some past relationships are more memorable than others, but they are recorded in our minds for future use. This event can be compared to a fresh coat of paint being applied over an old layer of paint or past experiences being covered up with new experiences. These experiences provide predictions on good and bad relationships. Feelings from past pains and frustrations are buried in the subconscious mind only to be awakened when familiar situations occur. The desires of the human heart are usually centered on finding true love with a person who can fully appreciate them. Each time a relationship is dissolved, and regardless of a reason, the heart will remain open for new opportunities to discover love.

(Story) How Old Relationships Can Impact A New Relationship

I counseled John in the past who had just ended a long-term relationship with Jane. However, John had recently found a new mate (April). The new relationship with April began with a mutual attraction and developed into a friendship. Their relationship could have been moving in a positive direction but was disrupted because of April's conduct. She did something that was like an experience John had with Jane. Two similar but different situations. However, John's decision was based on what happened in the past relationship with Jane. He did not try to resolve the conflict in a new way with April. John ends the relationship with April based on a previous bad experience. To make matters worse, John does not explain to April his reasoning for ending the relationship.

John's pain resurfaced from his past relationship with Jane. According to John, an issue with April reminds him of a similar matter with Jane. Even though Jane and April are different, John tries to circumvent more pain by ending the relationship with April prematurely. John's way of handling relationship conflict will always impact future relationships. This occurred because John was not able to let go of the pain endured from the past. John continuously guards his heart because of a shield of rejection. John's search for love will never live up to his expectations because his goal was to find a relationship without conflict. April is a victim left with a lot of questions not knowing all of John's emotional layers.

How can an individual allow pain from past relationships to go away? It is difficult to forget good or bad life experiences? Past experiences can be daunting; however, all situations and people are not the same. Every individual is unique. It is a mistake to label all men and women the same.

The human heart and mind are conditioned to learn and evolve from life experiences. This means our experiences allow us to make more informed decisions on new problems. Closure allows us to move on from the past. This means finding resolutions in your heart for guilt, blame, anger, and brokenness. Closure starts with forgiving the person who caused us pain. It is difficult to go through life with an open door to our heart. However, doors can be closed to pain and disrespect by cleansing the mind with positive energy. Positive energy involves having faith and belief in yourself.

The good Lord made everyone unique. There is no other person on earth with the exact characteristics. Therefore, close the door with positive energy. Speak to things that are true—you are wonderfully created. It is equally important to remove the guilt and close the door on the blame game. Do not allow your mind to create "what–if" scenarios triggering personal blame. It is a good idea to accept mistakes no matter who is to blame (you or your partner). This will begin the process of reshaping your future.

Chapter 3: The Conflict Between My Mind and Heart

A Dark Place

Have you ever wondered why so many struggles with heart break? Most people truly do not understand what a person must endure during this situation. It is easy for one to imply the relationship is over, so just move on. It is not just that easy for many to let go. It drives them to a dark place emotionally where they feel vulnerable and exposed. When a person has given their all to a relationship and it abruptly ends due to various reasons, it produces a natural wound that must be healed. The body when injured by a cut or bruise will immediately begin the process of healing. It will require careful treatment to protect the wound from infection while the body heals and leaves a scar. How does a person heal emotionally? The effect of an emotional wound produces an overload on the mind's capability to rationally adjust to the pain it must endure. This dark place full of despair has more questions than answers. This place where nothing matters, neither your socioeconomic nor educational background, the pain is the same. These feelings are real and cannot be utterly understood by many friends or family members. Those who experience this devastating pain must begin a healing process. The steps to recovery include acceptance and recognition of what occurred is real.

All romantic encounters shape us emotionally and can influence how we deal with future relationships. In most cases, our emotions support our innermost feelings. However, sometimes these feelings may not align with what has occurred. Oftentimes it is said that one cannot prevent the emotions of the heart. Every event that occurs during romantic encounter will be embedded in our minds, whether the outcome is good or bad. Ultimately, during our thought process, a logical solution will be created.

How do thought processes impact our romantic relationships? In a romantic relationship, our thought processes can be tricky. The reason relationships continue longer than expected is because our feelings may overrule our thoughts when facing an emotional event. Relationships may be extended because decisions are based on love instead of reason. As a result, this causes relationship conflict to be overlooked. To add to this matter, this type of uncertainty may entice some individuals to rethink their decisions. Ultimately, our emotions may alter our thought processes, signaling an overreaction to the event which can bring about a feeling of remorse.

Good thoughts, a need for love and emotional bonds, and our innermost feelings are created in our heart. Our hearts are filled with love and this is where secrets of passion are stored. Love connections are monitored by the heart and can influence subsequent relationship decisions. However, these love connections may cause mental and physical abuse, or even infidelity to be overlooked for the sake of love.

Our hearts and mind work together like business partners. This union is designed to protect us from abuse by providing early warning signs in romantic relationships.

The mind is the heart's business partner, and it protects the heart from abuse and provides an early warning sign in any relationship. Since the mind records all past and present relationships, it is aware when something is not right. During a bad situation, the mind sounds all the alarms and reminds the heart of a previous experience which resulted in a bad outcome. The heart will sometimes accept the advice and decide the mind must be correct. The question is: Do I follow my heart or my mind?

The answer is you follow them both, but you should avoid making snap decisions and you should think things through.

(Story) I Love My Mate but Hate Their Behavior

I provided counseling to a young couple who was in love and had started to build a family. Observers of their relationship would say she was in an abusive situation. Family members even stated she deserved better. She ignored their advice and continued to deal with his infidelity and abusive behavior. One thing about being an advisor is to assist a person you offer solutions to and allow them to make their decisions. This couple was in love and very young but very mature while the husband was not accepting his responsibility. Just knowing they loved each other was not enough to solve their problems. This created a dilemma for her, whether to follow her heart or her mind. For the relationship to improve, it required her husband to change his behavior. He was reluctant to change; however, he loved his wife and improved. Their marriage is still going strong today, but she had to assume the leadership role in the family. She was willing to live with his worst episodes and work through them as they occurred, to salvage her marriage. We often think marriage is a fairy tale, but the ones that last, work hard and love hard!

Making Good Decisions

It is one of the most challenging decisions to make, whether to end or continue a relationship. One person with the same situation forgave their partner after numerous conflicts and it blossomed into a wonderful relationship. Another terminated the relationship after a couple of conflicts and moved on. This is where good communication bears great benefits. If your soul mate listens and changes their behavior to improve, this implies they were concerned and value your love. In addition, if they refuse to communicate or change the offensive behavior, then you can consider their actions in your decision. Remember it is your life and decision, but God gave us an intelligent mind and eyes to see the truth. The worst-case scenario is to be in denial and accept abusive behavior as normal when it is contrary to the truth. This pattern of behavior will set you up for a showdown when your mind tells your heart "that is enough." This will lead to a major conflict which can lead to a mental health overload. I have heard many people say I am just stressed out in this relationship. It is these experiences that can carry over into new relationships.

The question often asked is: Who can I consult for good advice? Choose your friends carefully because many times their advice will be based on their past emotional experiences. It is important to know the decision is totally yours to consider. Best friends offer advice based upon their romantic experiences. Their advice may not be the right answer. Always think things through and consider all the facts before your emotions take charge and further complicate the situation. Meditate to help focus on your faith and relax. This will help you think things through. If a person is not telling the truth, eventually it will be uncovered. Just be patient and pray about the matter to ensure your decision is rational and based upon the facts.

Conflict Resolution

To develop great relationships, it will require conflict resolution skills. The best couples with long-term relationships have developed techniques regarding how to resolve conflicts. Hostility and verbal attacks will only escalate the problem. That is not to say that when you have experienced severe disappointment, you will just smile without emotions. During a conflict, anger builds with the feeling that this person disrespected you with their actions. Your emotions are high, while your mind has all kinds of thoughts based upon past experiences. To resolve the conflict, you must bring your emotions and mind to a calm place, so you can make a good decision. I often state that the strength of any relationship is based upon your ability to reconcile differences. Once you are emotionally and mentally in control, this will be the best time to discuss matters. The technique of conflict resolutions requires some meditation upon how your relationship has evolved and what problems exist. Once you identify all the problems, write them down. A good definition of problems must include what incidents or behaviors created emotional pain. The next step will be to identify what conduct or actions from your mate would solve the problem. During the discussion, your goal is to get your mate to agree with you or come to a mutual compromise. Your mate, upon agreement, understands this agreement is binding and you expect their compliance. Once you have all this information, you must discover if there are some underlying issues in your mate's mind that has created this problem. The discussion should include establishing ground rules, whereby your mate has the same opportunity to outline their issues and what could be a solution. The ground rules are set where no hostility will be allowed in the conference. Each person must remain calm and listen without theatrics.

Now the time has come to have this conference in a setting without distractions. Turn off cell phones, television, or anything that could interrupt your discussion. It is also important to be positive about the outcome and expectations. If you go into this discussion with hostility, anger, blame, condemnation, it may prevent conflict resolution. It is important in conflict resolution to stand your ground on behaviors which caused you emotional pain. Compromise is good but not at the expense of your mental health. Be open-minded and a good listener and allow your mate to explain their concerns. Also, when things start getting out of hand, redirect the conversation to the reason for the discussion. Men many times tend to shut down when they get upset and react based upon the tone of the conversation. Many women during counseling sessions inquire why men shutdown. Sometimes is a control mechanism for them in their minds which will not allow them to be out of control. It is also a sign the conversation is not productive and cannot be resolved during the present conversation. Each person must be genuine and be willing to compromise. If you follow this technique, you will really find out the source of emotional chains binding your mate's heart. This will also pinpoint the cause of their behaviors which are destructive to your relationship. Once agreements have been reached, write them down. This the most crucial part of this technique because there is a high probability these conflicts may reoccur. If they reoccur, you can recant the date and time you both agreed that such behavior is unacceptable. This type of resolution is only a guide to help to resolve conflict. It will work when two people who love one another can reason together to solve their problems.

I do not want to be hurt again!

When we have an injury, we cover it with a Band-Aid to protect it from being bruised again. This is our way to provide protection from being hurt again. There are not any acts or conducts which provide special protection from being hurt again. However, we can learn from prior experiences and observation from other relationships. What occurs is most people will put up protective guards and refuse to allow another person to get close again. Once the relationship develops to a point beyond a casual date, some will not allow it to flow but guard their heart from being hurt again. This fresh pain is a reminder of what occurred in their past.

Some refer to this as being bitter, disgruntled, and assuming all partners are the same as old ones. It brings back and relives the emotional rollercoaster and floods the mind with fear. No one desires to be hurt again, but to enjoy life, you cannot carry painful relationships into your future. Let it go because all people are not the same. These emotions are just like a fresh coat of paint to cover up a painful situation only to be uncovered in new relationships. It is not to say it causes a person to become bitter, but it has a great influence on the level of tolerance a person will develop moving forward in a new relationship. No rational person desires to repeat a bad situation; it is hopeful to learn from previous experiences to prevent them from reoccurring. It pays to be honest upfront when starting a new relationship so your partner can understand how you really feel. During many new relationships, a person does not understand the resistance and may take it personal and become unresponsive.

(Story) I Never Want to be Hurt Again!

I had a good friend who was married with two beautiful children. His wife was truly the love of his life. They both had successful careers and were well respected in their community. They purchased a home in an affluent neighborhood and appeared to be a happy family. He had two jobs working to provide for his family. Their marriage almost appeared perfect until he discovered she was having an affair with another man. He was devastated and heartbroken. His wife filed for divorce and he had to leave his home. The divorce was expensive and ruined him financially. The breakup impacted his credit and caused him to lose his home and many other valuable assets. While he suffered the embarrassment of divorce, the man who had an affair with his wife was driving the car he purchased for his wife and living in his home. I counseled him on many occasions to allow someone into his life again. The pain and humiliation were unbearable, and he decided never to marry again. He stated I cannot go through this pain again and would not allow any future relationships to build toward marriage. He recovered financially and led a prominent life. For many years he dated women who desired a permanent relationship, but he refused to fall in love and marry again. He never remarried until his death. This story reflects a man who could not forgive his mate or himself. Due to his pain he decided to remain in a safe place and guarded his heart to never be hurt again. He did not accept the fact that he had a lot to offer a new partner and all relationships are not the same.

A New Adventure

Moving forward is a new adventure, an opportunity to clear the past and all the negativity it created. Developing new friendships is important as you progress forward toward creating a new environment to find happiness. It is our past which helps us to evolve intellectually and emotionally so we become a stronger person. If you do not experience diversity how can you grow as a person. Many things in our past set us up for failure, but the fact really is that we must endure these experiences to face new situations. Your success and failures empower you as a person and allow you to assist others who face similar obstacles. Learn how to let go of failure and embrace it as a learning experience. Yes, we all have made mistakes and wonder how we could possibly be so dumb. A new adventure has an aroma of excitement mentally because again you have cast aside the past and look to the future with a new attitude. The resilience of the human spirit when broken and shattered has great restorative power when it focuses on the inner strength to believe that all things are possible. It is this energy that will drive a person from the couch of negativity to a place where hope can exist. It is a matter of putting the pieces back together and renewing your spiritual mind to a positive place.

Loving Yourself

Loving yourself is a self-caring attitude that life has value and requires action on your part to maintain love for yourself. Life is full of peaks and valleys, and we must grow to become our own number-one encourager. We spend a lifetime caring for others by sharing positive reinforcement through friendship and support. Each of us has so much love to share, so learn to appreciate your life and the positive events that occur each day. Loving yourself is not being conceited, it is just a self-appreciation for your life. You are your best cheerleader! An appraiser will always consider the uniqueness of an item's value when estimating its net worth. Consider out of the millions of people all over the world no one else has your exact DNA. Appreciate your uniqueness and celebrate the value of life. You cannot change the past, but your future is in your hands. Every person was wonderfully created with love and your life has immeasurable value. Take the time daily to appreciate your life. Your life requires positive energy to develop self-worth.

It is difficult to love yourself when you carry all of life's disappointment in your mind. To love yourself, celebrate your successes and learn from failures. Perfect people do not exist, but survivors always persevere through difficult situations. Loving yourself is accepting the things you cannot change and overcoming difficult trials and tribulations. negativities exist only in your mind; it must be discarded to preserve peace. It will attempt to control your emotions and drive you to a state of discouragement. Loving yourself after a disappointing failure can be mind-boggling if you allow blame to dominate your mind. These are the times when you commit your mind to balance success versus failure. Never let the bad occupy your mind more than the good. In other words, do not allow negativity to occupy your mind more than a good experience. Someone could easily say what is good when all has gone bad. To understand and appreciate the value of life, you must accept the bitter and the sweet. Life is not always bitter. I remember as a young man a sucker which was half sweet and half sour. You could start out with the bitter taste but after a while it got sweet. That is the way life can be; you can start out with a bitter experience, but just allow some time to pass, it will get sweeter.

Loving yourself is all about new beginnings! Just when darkness falls, we must endure the night, but early in the morning, the sun will rise to start a new day. Darkness is a time associated with the struggles of life. The unknown outcome of our trials creates a sense of darkness, fear, despair, and uncertainty, which impacts our peace of mind. It will conceal the forces which wage a war against our mind. Suffering is a nighttime experience, but these are the times to place value on life and count your blessings.

How can you love you? First is by understanding and removing the blame for failures during bad experiences. Pain is an adhesive and will cleave to you until you let it go. During stressful episodes, we project the appearance of having it all together only to cry out in frustration. Loving yourself is realizing your limitations and it is not your responsibility to please others which can be detrimental to your mental health. There is a champion inside of you that must be awakened. Freedom from the past requires you to elevate to a new level and rely on the inner strength to fight your way out.

Me-Time

How much time do you spend only on you? I cannot recollect all the recreational activities I have participated in over the years. My reward was to be with only my family and see my children's expressions while I attended their events. There is not enough time in the day to be all things to all people. In addition to these things, many parents maintain full-time employment. Pleasing others is a full-time job. The emotional energy spent to deal with others consumes the desire to focus on yourself. It is not a selfish act to invest time to self-reflect and satisfy your desires. It is important to remember the most important person that requires love and attention is YOU. If you are at your best, it sets the tone for you to fully appreciate those within your inner circle. It is difficult to provide love and support as a parent, caregiver, or spouse and still have time for you, but it can be done!

How do you find time for you? It is like any other thing that you do; it must be scheduled. Plan it out with the mind-set that it is well-deserved. So many people spend most of their life trying to make others happy only to realize two things—they must choose to be happy and happiness is a state of mind. In other words, many times your efforts cannot motivate them to be happy. Me-time is your time to take that trip or slip away to a place just to strengthen your inner person. This time can be shared with a special friend or just by being alone. Your best friend lives inside of you. You as an individual; understand your needs and too much time is spent relying on others to make you feel excited and full of life. Be motivated and spend quality time focusing on mentally unloading all the stressors in your life and appreciate being you.

Me-time is the time taken to regenerate your emotions and get away from the mundane routines to relax and enjoy life. You deserve it, so plan it. Remember it does not require major expenditures; it could simply be time set aside in your life just for you.

Positive Energy

We all have experienced failures which were completely our fault, but that's life and we learn from these trials. In addition, we have been around individuals with negative attitudes who discourage others. If you allow negative thoughts to mentally dominate your mind, they will steal your energy. Most people would immediately redirect a stranger who made negative comments about you. It is important to control negative energy and redirect it into positive energy. It is often said talking to yourself may reflect a mental dysfunction, but you are your best cheerleader. To enjoy a healthy mental state, you need to control the flow of energy through your mind. Your mind reacts to the thoughts and impulses from daily-life situations and this impacts your state of mind. We cannot control the tragedies associated with our life. We can only react to negative and positive situations. It is extremely easy to deal with positive experiences because they bring pleasure and make us appreciate the good things happening in our life. It is the negative experiences which produce stress and present obstacles we must overcome. Negative energy causes our mind to rationalize how to handle what we just experienced. Since the problems do not have an immediate solution, our mind continues through the thought process to find a resolution to release from worry. The most powerful tool we have is our faith which produces hope. Hope is the positive energy that God gives to those who need strength to overcome bad experiences. The power to overcome negative energy relies upon your ability to reinforce your mind with positive energy.

Chapter 4: Guard your Heart

Once you have dealt with the past, the future seems bright, but your heart and mind bear the remembrance of past experiences. It is because of these factors that you subconsciously protect yourself by building a mind-set— "do not get hurt twice." As new relationships begin to emerge, and synergy builds in a new relationship, the emotional breaks begin to slow down the process by means of caution flags. Due to past relationships, limits are placed upon your new relationship, many times based upon facts that do not exist in the new relationship but did in the previous one. A guard is placed upon the heart to prevent it from ever being in a place of vulnerability. Although a person still believes in love and romance, they will not fully commit to a new relationship without guarding their heart. This is a normal process after dealing with a prior relationship that was dissolved. To build a new relationship, a person must not remain in a permanent mode of resistance.

A new love can be destroyed quickly if a partner determines the relationship is not progressing and has no future. It is during these times many are afraid of committing to a new partner and withhold their innermost feelings which will not allow them to build a relationship. A healthy relationship is built upon trust and friendship. One of the greatest hindrances to moving forward is overcoming the fear of being hurt again. You can do all the right things to build the perfect relationship and it can dissipate into thin air overnight. The greater pain is not to even try but remain in a mind-set of protection and not allowing anyone to love you. Fear is a tormentor; therefore, overcome any fear by believing in yourself to be strong enough to get over your past. Your future is exciting and waiting on you to create the environment for joy and happiness.

There is no guarantee in relationships; it is a challenge that tests your resolve. There are several things you can do to prepare for a new relationship:

1. Believe in yourself;

2. Bury the past;

3. Learn from your mistakes;

4. Trust your instincts;

5. Allow your new relationship time to build.

It is difficult to move forward in any relationship unless you have the confidence in yourself to find the right person. It is essential to dismiss all negative criticism of fault due to failed relationships and understand even good relationships will dead end. The good Lord made you intelligent and so beautiful that no other person in the world is just like you. Things of true value are related to their uniqueness. Like a precious diamond, whose value is based upon its beauty and uniqueness. Confidence requires courage and accepting the things you cannot change and moving forward with a new attitude on life. In addition, it is important to have closure from past relationships. It is impossible to forget what caused you pain, but refuse to allow it to occupy your time. You must believe there is a new, exciting person waiting for you in the future. Be optimistic and learn how to enjoy those around you such as your family and friends. Enjoy just being alone and not having someone else as a requirement for happiness. True love will find you but when it does be prepared and have the right attitude for it to develop.

The best way to prevent something from occurring again is to learn from your mistakes. It may be true the person who caused you pain really took advantage of the situation. However, there had to be warning signs that were ignored to allow things to get out of control. If this situation happens, listen to those who really care about your well-being. A best friend may offer an objective opinion. Notate possible mistakes and learn from them. Many times, these warnings come in just as a feeling of uncertainty which sometimes is simply ignored. Learn to embrace your intuition and follow through on things that do not appear to make sense. Trust your instincts and guard your heart with common sense. As you embark on a new relationship give it time to build. No one desires to be hurt again, but love is like a rose plant which appears simple that produces a beautiful colorful bloom.

Let the Healing Process Begin

To assist your loved ones, many times, they must get healed from the pain from broken relationships. Due to unresolved disputes, many loved ones are separated emotionally and refuse to communicate with each other. The best advice is trying to work through problems in life so when you are faced with having to assist a loved one, these bad feelings will not come to surface. However, if this does happen, you must resolve your differences. Forgiveness is simply letting go of the pain and frustration that you are allowing to live in your mind. I understand words and actions speak, but the number one question is: Is the pain worth carrying around with you for the rest of your life? If you forgive this person and yourself regarding whatever happened, then from that moment on you can have peace. Understand peace is not based upon the action of another person but how you feel about the situation. If you have forgiven yourself and the other person, you will have mental peace. The other person may continue with resentment and allow the pain to fester in their minds. You however have moved to a new level.

True forgiveness does not erase the bad experience from your memory. The power is in the release when you simply say it from the heart, "I forgive them and myself for the pain we both have shared."

Forgiveness allows you to move forward with the right attitude toward your loved one. These situations are not easy because in life I know some of your greatest pain is from broken relationships. It is difficult but it can be accomplished and be a true test of your resolve. A new beginning is the refusal to allow anyone to take you back to through that experience. The greatest gift in the Bible is love.

Normally when a person is injured physically, the healing process will begin immediately. This human body is designed to restore itself if proper care is being provided. Fresh pain from broken relationships create emotional stress. The mind will recall past experiences especially issues which were not resolved. The healing process affects many people so differently. The worst mistake is to assume all people handle stressful experiences the same way. Each person must go through the healing process based upon their life experiences and recovery timeframes will vary. We look for answers regarding how to move on and overcome this bad experience. The answer is a biblical one!

Forgiveness is the first step to overcome pain. It is not easy, but it is necessary for your mental state of mind. You must elevate your mind-set to refuse to allow that situation to affect your life in a negative manner. Just like an open wound, it requires cleaning, antibiotics, protecting, and daily caring. The pain from the wound reminds you it still not healed completely and cannot be used at its full strength. An emotional wound has the same characteristics, it requires the mind to be cleaned with positive energy. It must have protection and daily care. Some comments from anyone who has been betrayed is I cannot forgive them, it is too painful. The basic medical relief for pain is to remove the source and treat the symptom. Healing cannot occur without removing the source of the pain. Pain medication can help relieve the pain, but it does not remove the source.

Forgiveness is not just going through the motions to convince yourself, but it requires an acceptance of the experience that caused the pain. The second step of acceptance requires dealing with the blame and shame. It can be difficult for a person who caused the pain to fully understand the emotional impact on the other person.

The Release

To accept what occurred, it truly means you stop the blame and shame game. What has occurred was the result of many issues, and if you are looking for blame, you can find it everywhere. Blame is a tormentor which creates intense frustrations against another person or oneself. It can dominate the thoughts of the human mind and control emotional impulses to punish someone. The only persons living in pain are the ones who continually search for a person to blame. Many times when no one is available, it is easy to blame oneself. This is the worst type of pain when you blame yourself because it allows your mind and thought process to continuously inflict pain to the point of depression. Acceptance is simply stating this bad situation has occurred in my life due to another person's or my own actions. Once acceptance has occurred, then your mind can rest from the torment of blame. This is the beginning of the healing process.

The next step is to redirect your thoughts to accept what has occurred and to move forward. You can accept what occurred and still feel discouraged. In other words, you may go a week without a negative emotional experience but somehow something triggers fresh pain. Remember how we described how a natural wound requires cleaning daily to prevent infection. If the wound is not cleaned properly, another infection can occur which could be worse than the original condition. The mind requires daily cleaning and restoration to remain healthy. How can you control the thoughts that travel through your mind? Thoughts just happen without warning, and once they occupy your mind, they impact your emotions. If you embrace the emotion of sorrow, it creates a depressing mood. However, if you reject it with positive energy, your mind will move in that direction. To impact your feeling, it will require control and redirection of your negative thoughts. Do not allow negative or painful thoughts to control your mind. Let us review the steps so far: forgive, accept, and redirect your thoughts.

The fourth step is release. Release is letting go of all the pain and frustration that has occupied your mind. This condition will keep you in a dark place unless it is rejected. Release signifies that something has been held captive which desires freedom. Bondage on the other hand indicates a situation of being in captivity. The power of bondage means to be isolated in a place where no one can help. Bondage occurs when a situation is held within the mind where no one can help unless it has been released so freedom can come in. To release something within your mind, you must be able to openly discuss your circumstances and innermost feelings. Releasing these emotional pains and frustrations take away the pressure of disguising your true feelings. As many say, the truth will set you free. During times of difficulty, we can become some of the greatest pretenders who falsely indicate we are strong and in control. The truth of the matter is that you are just one tear away from crying. This emotional release is not a sign of weakness but strength. Release is a crystal-clear statement that you will not let this pain defeat your spirit. It is a battle cry of a victorious person who overcame a dark pain. The agony was real, but it did not defeat me. Release is admission of being wounded in the battle but still emerging victorious. Victory over emotional pain is without bitterness, guilt or shame. This release is declaring a new day has begun through a challenging emotional experience. It is a new you who is in touch with their emotional side displaying a bright, beautiful future ready for life and declaring that the best is yet to come.

Now it is time to release and let go of the pain. Pain is something that is carried in the mind of those who have been hurt. Our minds will continue to review the events and continuously promote discomfort and reminders of what occurred. This release is not about who was right or wrong, but it deals with acceptance and releasing yourself from the consequences. One thing about yesterday you cannot change is what occurred. We can only impact the future with decisions made each day. The decision to release yourself requires a removal of guilt and shame. It is impossible to forget your pass, but it is possible to forgive and release the pain. To mentally release a situation, you must be ready to move on with your life. It is unfortunate bad things happen to good people. Our faith is a powerful force which allows a believer to transfer pain to a higher source. The foundation of our faith is a release from worldly concerns by believing our God can help us overcome our pain. It is important to understand release is not simply a one-day thing for everyone. Many can release their pain and move forward, but for others, it may be a continuous battle to overcome. Release is a proclamation regarding your future. It is a mental and spiritual stand against the past pain which occupies your mind. Peace of mind can only manifest when you feed it good thoughts and reflect upon the positive events in your life. In addition, it requires an admission to the truth regarding what truly just occurred. You call it just like it happened regardless of who was at fault. The warning signs many times were there, but simply ignored. It is not a situation of rekindling anger but a situation of just accepting the truth.

Celebrate Your Deliverance

This nightmarish experience had an impact on your emotional state of mind and spirituality. It did not destroy your life but made you stronger. Even if the memory of what you endured still resonates in your mind. It was by faith and a strong will to survive that you achieved victory over this trial. After all the pain and humiliation, sleepless nights, and tears of frustration, it is time to celebrate your deliverance. It is not about what others think only you know what occurred. It is time to celebrate; you have achieved victory. It is not about finding another partner but recognizing the spirit of a champion that dwells on the inside. This celebration is not foolishness or to point a finger at those who caused the pain. It is about you being fully recovered and ready for a new beginning. No more pain and frustration but a new you has emerged who has peered in the face of this horrific situation and declared victory. How do you celebrate? It can be a simple thing like taking yourself out on a date to enjoy the moment. True happiness comes from within a person. This emotional release is not a sign of weakness but of strength. A release is a crystal-clear statement; you will not let this pain defeat your spirit. It is a battle cry of a victorious person who overcame a dark pain. The agony was real, but it did not defeat you. Release is an admission of being wounded in battle but still emerging victorious—victory over emotional pain without bitterness, guilt, or shame. This release is declaring a new day has begun through a challenging, emotional experience. It is a new you who is touch with their emotional side with a bright beautiful future. It is in a declaration the best is yet to come.

Developing New Standards in Relationships

Compatibility

It is often said a reason for divorce or termination of a relationship is the couple was just not compatible. What is compatibility and why is it important. Some think *well my mate is an outdoorsman and loves to hunt and I dislike the outdoors and prefer the quiet life of reading a book.* That is not what compatibility is all about; couples can have totally different hobbies and interests but still have a wonderful, sharing relationship. Compatibility is how you function as a couple by sharing trust and your innermost feelings. Have you heard that opposites attract? These differences can be an issue depending on your tolerance for what your mate enjoys. The important part of compatibility is when you understand that your relationship has priority over all personal interest.

The Compatibility Guide

The compatibility guide below is designed based upon interests and questions based upon feedback from individuals who have been successful in building relationships. Remember you are the decision-maker in your relationships based upon the standards set by you.

Compatibility Test Scale of 1 to 10

Not based upon any scientific facts or behavior analysis only for recreational opinion

Scale of 1 to 10

1. Is my significant other honest?

Scale of 1 to 10

2. How often does my mate give me a compliment?

Scale of 1 to 10

3. Is my mate financially independent?

Scale of 1 to 10

4. Is my mate a moral person?

Scale of 1 to 10

5. If my life were at stake, would they come to rescue me?

Scale of 1 to 10

6. If my mate proposed marriage, would I say yes?

Scale of 1 to 10

7. Can my mate control their temper?

Scale of 1 to 10

8. Can I live with the worst habits my mate has?

Scale of 1 to 10

9. Do you feel your mate is faithful?

Scale of 1 to 10

10. Does my mate and I have common interests?

Scale of 1 to 10

Result of Scores

The maximum score is 100 points. The idea is simple, if your average scores are below 50, consider working to improve your relationship. A score above 80 is a positive score with potential based upon the questions. These are common-sense-type questions. However, there are many other factors to consider in which one bad response may overrule others. The worst mistake many people make in relationships is being blinded by love and ignoring the obvious serious problems. Love is powerful, but it will not resolve behavior issues. The idea that you can change a person can lead to a disastrous outcome. The truth is a person must recognize they have a problem and be willing to pursue whatever avenue necessary to help them change.

A simple test does not truly define the potential of a person but reflects their present character. The problem being that many individuals are not mature enough to cope with a serious relationship. The reason maybe they are not ready or have never experienced a true, loving relationship. This person has potential if they are willing to build a relationship. The characteristics required to grow and develop. Please understand those in long-term relationships still encounter episodes of misunderstandings. If you are looking for a perfect relationship, understand upfront no one is perfect including you. The strength of relationships is their ability to overcome conflict.

Chapter 5: How to Salvage My Marriage

Based upon the Centers for Disease Control and Prevention's(CDC) National Center for Health Statistics the U. S. marriage rate for (45 reporting states and D. C) from 2000 to 2018 was 6.5 per 1000 total population which is the lowest rate in over 18 years (CDC Marriage and Divorce, 2003). In addition, the divorce rate is 2.9 per 1,000 population.

According to an article in *The Balance*, "How Long Do Average U. S. Marriages Last? (Lake, 2020), the average length of a marriage is around 8 years. The average age of divorce is 30. The author of the article estimates that 60% of divorces are between the ages of 25–29 (Lake, 2019). In addition, 62% of second marriages and 73% of third marriages end in a divorce. Cases surveyed by Certified Financial Analyst state the reasons for divorce as follows: basic compatibility, 43%; infidelity, 28%; financial, 23%; and emotional and/or physical abuse, 5.8% (CDFA 2013).

The warning signs of a marriage with significant issues are when two people who made a commitment begin to grow apart. This relationship which began out of a memorable romantic encounter evolved to marriage. First it must be understood every marriage requires effort, commitment, trust, communication, and the ability to reconcile differences. Many factors can create problems in a marriage such as infidelity and financial problems. Marriage is a lifetime commitment that must be taken seriously, especially when the honeymoon period is over. It is unfortunate many couples enter a marriage for the wrong reasons. This creates a problem when a couple does not know what the expectations and requirements are for a lasting relationship. Marriage is about sharing and understanding how your mate responds to divisive issues. You must give them value and the understanding to build a relationship based upon mutual respect. A lasting relationship is built upon trust. It is when trust is violated when problems occur and cause conflict in a marriage. I have counseled many couples with marital issues to help them overcome their differences. My advice about infidelity is that it does not have to end your relationship if there is a sincere sense of remorse. It requires willingness from your partner to change their behavior. People will always dictate how they would react, but they are not in your situation.

(Story) Compromise Leads to Reconciliation

I counseled a couple that had been married for over 20 years. They were a fun-loving couple with children and appeared to be happy. His wife asked for advice on how to salvage their marriage. She simply stated her husband was continuously unfaithful and despite her forceful confrontations, he never changed. She indicated she had enough but loved her husband and was willing to work things out if possible. Her consideration also included her desire to keep her family intact, so the children would have a strong family structure.

The first step was to setup a meeting to establish ground rules with her husband where they both would be under control and refrain from emotional outbursts. Their conversation would address the immediate problems they were facing. They both would be able to address issues which impacted their marriage without repercussions. My suggestion was to describe the minimum requirement which her husband must display for their marriage to continue. In addition, she would have parameters which must be adhered to or consequences will be enacted upon. These concerns must be a written agreement to which both agreed to comply. She completed her agreement and setup a meeting with her husband to discuss concerns with specific ground rules of conduct by both sides. Her first issue to address was his infidelity and ascertain whether he had remorse and the willingness to seriously renew their relationship. He confessed his infidelity and desired to do whatever was necessary to rebuild his marriage. The important part of his confession was his wife accepted it and made a true admission of forgiveness. Reconciliation cannot work properly without forgiveness. If a person constantly reminds their mate of their faults such as infidelity, it becomes impossible to move forward. Remember marriage is built upon a close friendship based upon trust. Once these bonds are broken, a couple must go back to the basics of marriage and become friends again. It is almost like dating to rekindle a relationship by demonstration of an effort made in good faith. She had an agreement which stated if he desired to continue their marriage, he must be faithful and a future conduct in this manner would result in a divorce. He was required to sign it, so he clearly understood the seriousness of her concerns. He in turn addressed his concerns with his wife in an open conversation with the understanding she would take his issue seriously and adjust to improve their relationship. They also discussed how to spend more quality time with each other. One important issue was whenever one person's behavior violated the agreement, they would redirect their partner to the original commitment. This couple managed their agreement as their relationship improved over the years. They both became strong supporters of their children and joined a local church. As time passed, they became grandparents and enjoyed spending quality time with each other. They improved their relationship by ensuring they spent quality time with each other by taking vacations together and attending functions as a couple. If a person's conduct is causing you pain, it must be addressed with a good, clear understanding. Sometimes silence does not bring peace, but only paints over the true feeling with the hope that things will change. Change does not occur on its own, but requires an open dialogue with a clear plan to correct the problem. Conflict resolution requires both partners to listen to each other's concerns and be willing to compromise.

Why Do Partners Cheat in Their Relationship?

This is a million-dollar question: Why people cheat on each other. According to an article, Why do People Cheat in Relationships? (Raypole, 2019) According to a 2017 study of 259 women and 213 men. The results indicated several reasons were anger or revenge, falling out of love, situational factors, opportunity, unmet needs, sexual desire, wanting variety, and low self-esteem.

One of the main reasons based upon my experiences for divorce or broken relationships is infidelity. First explore the damage caused by infidelity. Infidelity impacts a person for the rest of their life, when you have absolutely loved a person and faithfully given them all your love, only to be emotionally blindsided. This emotional pain paints a picture of being violated, foolish, mental anguish and anger. To understand a person's heartfelt love, recognize you are one of the few people they have allowed to enter their innermost being. One does not easily enter this sensitive and emotional place which is only restricted for those you really love. It is not a passing relationship or a friend with benefits. But one based upon trust. Once a person enters this special place, they receive all the love and passion they have to offer. In this area only, your relationship and everything you represent makes their life complete. Once true love is released from their heart it accepts your entrance into their life. Emotionally they are in a good place being in your presence. This significant commitment causes them to trust and consider you the best over all the rest. Infidelity creates a type of pain which is excruciating and should not be taken lightly. People in love have fun and it is exciting when the simplest of things bring joy, such as sitting in the park or watching a movie in bed. So why do people cheat. Well look at most common explanations: lack of sex, growing apart, increased stress due to children, and financial problems. The truth of the matter is that all couples experience problems but not all commit infidelity. One of the most common places people initiate relationships is their place of employment, group meetings and frequent acquaintances. Remember, relationships begin with friendship where two people simply enjoy being with each other. Partners who begin to build friendships outside of their marriage allow it to develop beyond a normal friendship. This can develop into emotional adultery a romantic bond which ties two people in a dangerous relationship. They can become sexually attracted and do not consider the consequences of their action. In addition, they find qualities in another person which are not common in their marriage. This will lead to blaming their partner for some inadequacies which create a feeling of neglect, so they seek satisfaction through another person. Couples must also be aware that each day their mate receives attention from the opposite sex. They simply chose not to act upon the invitation. Be sure you are the one who starts your mate day off with a compliment and the assurance that they are special. There are those who want to have their cake and eat it too, which means they desire multiple partners. The absolute truth about infidelity is a person makes a conscious decision to enter a forbidden relationship. Once this door has been opened, it will impact their present relationship once it has been exposed. Infidelity will create an emotional discord and distance in a relationship. A person who attempts to love two people at the same time will leave something lacking. Their infidelity will be providing some signs which are often ignored. Once this infidelity is discovered, it can devastate the foundation of a marriage. The knowledge of this indiscretion will emotionally drain their partner's mental state in the attempt to figure out why this situation has occurred. Infidelity has an impact on the complete family structure when a relationship has been destroyed, especially upon the children. The person who commits infidelity does not fully understand the risk that produces devastating consequences. The heart of a person they loved, and their offspring severed in way that paints a picture of painful memories which last forever. Infidelity that leads to divorce does not leave a winner but creates despair.

It is understood some relationships are dysfunctional, and couples remain together without solving their problems. Who can judge why people remain in a dysfunctional situation? It is their choice to decide their tolerance level. There is hope if two people can become friends again. They must reconnect with truth and honesty and rebuild the basic foundations required to renew their relationship. It is the willingness between two people that decides what they can accept. This is the primary reason for our high divorce rate because a couple's tolerance levels for indiscretions of any form have exceeded beyond repair. The difficult part is they carry the layers of emotional pain from past experiences into their next relationship. I have been married over 40 years and understand my marriage still requires work and dedication to ensure a happy home. Relationships under pressure are vulnerable and can easily be broken behind the trials and tribulations of life. Those who have marriages such as mine have a common thread—they are good friends with their mates, and many have a spiritual bond aligned with their faith. The early emotional and physical attractions will not die but become more refined. This simply means you are on a lifetime date. The energy and excitement during the dating stage make a relationship sizzle. It creates an atmosphere of love and companionship. A marriage must be cultivated by each partner's willingness to a lifetime commitment. This requires a desire to overcome obstacles which occur to create conflict. It is the simple differences—being more patient and less reactive. It requires an open dialogue but with a common goal to work together. During conflict, avoid packing a suitcase and departing. Ensure you stay at home in the heat of a fight, even if you sleep on the couch. The best of couples have had moments of conflict but are willing to work through their differences.

Passion and Intimacy

I often have received request from one of the partners in a marriage regarding the lack of passion. During the honeymoon part of the relationship, intimacy was rampant and emotional expression of true love was exhibited with strong acts of affection. The passion of the relationship is the most important fulfillment of marriage. A strong outward and inward expression of heartfelt love is a requirement for it to flourish. This passion is also fueled by adding children to the mix which acts as the fiber that puts purpose in a marriage. Passion is the fuel which ignites intimacy. Sex is important, but it requires foreplay to create the atmosphere for romance. One of the common problems in a marriage is the lack of sexual activity. Sex is a divine creation for the purpose of enjoyment and reproduction. Sexual desire is a natural instinct to please their spouse and is necessary for marital bliss. The common complaints about sex are the lack of frequency, passion, and satisfaction. It is difficult for anyone to think about sex when they are dealing with mental abuse and an uncertain future. It is your responsibility to create the environment for intimacy. When is the last time you let your mate know they are sexy and appealing? Try new things and do not be so predictable. Ask your mate about what excites them in moments of intimacy. If you are having problems, do not use sex as a weapon. This opens the door for temptation. If you have too many distractions at home, rent a room for the weekend.

Parenting and Marriage

Parenting is a demanding responsibility which requires commitment and a balance between children and the marriage. This balance is finding time to spend with children and satisfying the needs of your spouse. The pressure on marriages are two-pronged, with the first phase being raising children and the second being the children maturing and leaving home. The requirements of family include employment and recreational activities which are time-consuming. Couples find joy in supporting family outings which add value to life and create memories of fun-filled experiences. So, couples find it hard to make time for each other after a long day's work come home to cook and care for the children. What left is no energy you just want to prepare for bed. It is important to understand there are emotional and physical needs which must be met. Despite all the soccer mom and father duties schedule time for each other. If you do not schedule time, it will not happen because other events suddenly demand your attendance. Find a babysitter and buy three roses and spread the petals from the front door to the bedroom.

As the children mature and eventually branch out, the empty nest syndrome does have an effect. The family structure changes from built in activities with children to spending time with your mate. It is during these times the marriage must be rekindled with passion. Passion is critical for survival in a marriage. The number-one complaint from couples is the lack of passion. Intimacy and passion are two different things.

Passion Story

I met a couple many years ago. The husband was a strong, tall, vibrant man and his wife was a beautiful blond with blue eyes. They adored each other. Her husband was involved in a car accident and was permanently paralyzed. Due to his condition, he was restricted to a wheelchair which required his wife to provide full-time care. His wife continued to love him and provide for his care with grace as though his physical condition was not a factor. Considering she was still young and attractive and could have easily found a reason to leave her husband due to his disability. I met them about 10 years later and she continued to care for her differently able husband with compassion and heartfelt love. While I observed their relationship, it gave me insight into a definition of true love and commitment. The way she treated him was as if he were the love of her life and even his disability could not tarnish what she felt in her heart. Passion and intimacy are important, but passion can last even when intimacy fades.

Married couples must not allow passion to die in their relationships, and often when this occurs, so will intimacy. Passion is what makes the person you love the most important part of your life. It is not assuming a person understands how you feel about them but reassuring them with a sense of pleasure being in their presence daily. It is to notice and appreciate the little things and never allow your relationship to die. When passions diminish in a relationship, it becomes cold, dysfunctional, and lacks intimacy, and the marriage can develop into a financial arrangement. It is common that when a couple is in this situation, intimacy becomes a thing of the past. Couples can be married and living in the same house for years in separate bedrooms without intimacy but appear to be a happy couple in the presence of others. Their marriage becomes dysfunctional, and passion and intimacy do not exist in the relationship. This sets the marriage up for failure and opens the door for extramarital affairs which further destroy their relationship.

Fan the Flames

One thing about a natural fire is like a marriage at its peak it is hot and sizzles. When firewood burns, it sizzles and pops, providing heat and a relaxing sound. As the fire burns, it slowly loses its power and the vibrant flame slowly moves to a flicker and soon turns into ashes. Many times, this is a description of a strong marriage fueled by passion and intimacy but slowly due to lack of this energy loses its intensity. One thing about a fire even when the flame fades to white ashes heat stills exist under the coal. This fire can be ignited if the coals are stimulated by fanning the flames. It is noticeable that by stimulating the ashes and adding more wood, the fire rekindles. A new exciting relationship can be restored from the ashes if passion and intimacy can be restored. If a couple takes the necessary steps and refuses to allow their relationship to die by taking steps to rekindle the flames of passion. How can this be done when so much has happened? Well it starts with communication and a renewed commitment. Communication requires a better understanding of how your mate feels about the relationship. In addition, it is their willingness to change the marital atmosphere by exhibiting new energy with passion and genuine concern for a successful relationship. It requires setting new standards of spending quality time with each other and listening with concern to your mate's desires. Simply draw a line in the sand and refuse to accept the situation as it stands. Establish a meeting time and make your intentions clear. Change your attitude to compromise in order to improve the relationship. Seek counseling and professional guidance if necessary, to restore your marriage.

Divorce

One of the most devastating events which can impact the family is divorce. It ranks as a top stressor, ranking just below loss of a loved one. It is another layer of emotional paint to cover the couple and their children with events that impact their future relationships. Every relationship has peaks and valleys. For a marriage to take place, two people decide to make a commitment to build a relationship through holy matrimony. We know marriages are built and established on friendship, and just like losing a good friend so is divorce. Despite the cause of a divorce, it leaves a lasting memory in the mind of both persons. Divorce is the conclusion of a relationship. Simply stated it is a failed relationship. No one wins; there is not a victory lap even though it brings joy it also leaves the real feeling this once loveable union ended in a negative manner. Someone gave the best of their love which was rejected and abused. They must deal with these feelings for them to move forward with a new beginning.

Chapter 6: How to Build a Lasting Relationship

According to an article in weddingstats.org, the average length of a relationship is 4.9 years before marriage (Average 2020). In 2020, the average age of marriage for a woman is 27.1 years and men 29.2 years (John, 2020).

I have been married over 40 years to the same beautiful woman. It is the most wonderful feeling to have a relationship which has lasted through raising my children and now grandchildren. It takes work and patience to build a lasting relationship.

My journey started as a child because my mother trained me to respect women. I obeyed her until the age of 16, when I vowed to never marry and be a player for life. Just like the average young man, I desired to impress young girls with trendy apparel and good looks. This is normal for most young men during the dating cycle to display affection and develop relationships. My uttermost desire was to find a perfect mate to date on a regular basis. The search began in high school to find love, only to lose it foolishly overnight. It was exciting to pursue the young ladies and to receive their attention. This lasted until I graduated from high school and entered the Air Force at the age of 18. Life began to change and relationships were not just simply courtship, but each one was serious and had consequences. Dating required faithfulness to your mate and love was demonstrated by actions and conduct. I had to learn many lessons about building a relationship. Just like many other young men, I went through various relationships seeking one true love. It was a learning experience to determine the differences between fantasy and love. Learning what was appealing to the eye did not translate into a person with a pleasant personality. In addition, learning the lesson of love can be wonderful and painful. So many lessons to learn—breaking up and making up. I had to experience betrayal and being heartbroken. These experiences, just like layers of paint, are covered up, but they are forever alive in your heart. Despite all the bad relationships, your heart desires and expects to find a person who will fulfil all your needs. As you grow older, you seek relationships with substance. I clearly remember just praying and making a deal with God that if he gave me my soul mate, I would dedicate my life to him. While serving in the military based in the Aleutian Islands, Alaska, which was around 4 miles long and 2 miles wide. During my tour, it allowed me time to focus on the things that were important. I was isolated from society for one full year which allowed me to mature as a man and identify with my innermost feeling. Once this tour was completed, I was looking for love for the right reasons. Upon my return from this remote military assignment to regular society, I needed to make some adjustments. Due to this remote assignment I had not seen any children or an American car for over 1 year. It was my plan to change my focus from "seek and devour" to "build friendships." It caused me to mature for the first time and focus on the kind of relationship I desired to develop with a woman. Once discharged from the military, I returned to my hometown with a plan to complete college and find love. I still had some growing pains and lessons to learn.

I clearly remember one Saturday night out riding with one of my high school classmates, we pulled up to a restaurant to buy food. A brown Monte Carlo was parked adjacent to us full of young ladies. The driver caught my eye and I remembered meeting her years ago in high school. I made several comments and requested for her to get out of the car to obtain a better view. We exchanged phone numbers and made a tentative date to meet the next day. This was the beginning of our journey. We developed a great friendship, going out on several dates. I enrolled into college and found employment. We would visit each other during lunch and on the weekends.

In addition, we started meeting each other's families and just had fun. As our relationship began to develop, our friendship began to evolve. At times we had our differences but we quickly made up and did not harbor ill feelings. We simply enjoyed each other's company. She was beautiful inside and had a great personality. Our relationship continued to grow over the next several months. I still had areas in my life which required improvement; however, my feelings for her were true. I was 22 and she was 21 when we fell in love. It was one Saturday night when I stared into her eyes and recognized the most beautiful woman I had ever seen. I decided she would be my wife and would not spend another day without her in my life.

I was a college student and working full-time. Due to my financial commitments, I was not able to afford an expensive ring. The ring I purchased was so small but it represented a lifetime commitment. My plan was to propose to her on Saturday night. I remember going down on one knee and asking her to be my wife. She smiled and said, "Yes, I will marry you." This occurred after we had been dating about 9 months. Finally, I had found my true love. We planned a church wedding during the summer. The wedding was wonderful and my dream had come true. Both of us were so excited to move into our new duplex to start our lives. Our first living room set was a used one and was purchased for $100. It consisted of a couch and a loveseat. The couch had 3 legs and the fourth leg was missing, so we used 2 bricks to hold it up. We were so excited to be together, every day being full of puppy love. The honeymoon period was a time when you just cannot get enough of each other. Life was full, and we enjoyed spending time doing everything together. However, deep down inside I had the feeling that something was missing in my life. There was a void inside of me where I struggled to find peace. I remember going to church with my mother-in-law and had a sense I needed more in my life. This day turned out to be a special day because I committed my life to Christ. This experience changed my life. It was through this experience I learned how to love myself and my wife with a deeper love. In addition, it caused me to mature spiritually and genuinely love my wife in a special way. Our marriage blossomed and we both dedicated our lives to the ministry. No matter what type of faith you have, it must be demonstrated daily in the way you treat others. Our marriage has endured and blossomed for 40 years and counting. Some think marriage is like a family show, but it truly evolves around developing a better understanding of your mate. You must respect her as your equal and show her through your actions her love is valuable.

Tips to Develop Resolutions—Forgiveness

I have stated that a relationship starts with friendship which is built upon trust. Whenever trust is violated, it damages the foundation of the relationship. My first tip is to maintain your marriage just like best friends. Well, a good friend is thoughtful, honest, and will not leave your side when you need them the most. We know even the best of friends have disagreements and sometimes say things they really do not mean. Good friends are patient and use the greatest tool to any relationship, which is forgiveness. No one desires to lose a good friend and are willing to defend against every situation that threatens their friendship. Forgiveness in a relationship rises to a new level above who is right or wrong but focuses on solutions to restore and resolve the conflict. Many couples spend more time seeking an apology than a solution. Therefore, so many people continually commit the same acts and apologize because the problem has not been solved. Normally conflict results in partners not speaking and behaving like two strangers living in the same home. Forgiveness is the ultimate test of love. The second tip is many individuals solve conflict by running away, avoidance simply attempting to ignore the problems until it gets better. Doing conflicts do not run away from home unless it has become a dangerous situation. Try to manage the conflict, remain at home even when tensions are high. Anger affects each person differently, so get to know how your mate handles anxiety. If a situation has gotten out of hand and your mate is upset allow them some time to process what has occurred. Seek the right time to address your concerns and ensure you are in control of your anger. Many couples during these times ponder if their mates will ever change.

Personal Improvement Plans

You can spend a lifetime trying to change people only to recognize the only person you can profoundly change is YOU. Therefore, rather than trying to establish a personal improvement plan for your mate. Start to change the person who can impact the most, which is YOU. Regardless of everything, your mate is not considering the fact that you are not perfect and right in every situation. Examine your behavior to identify areas of improvements. Most of the time it is easiest to pinpoint everything your mate is not. Many couples focus on their mate's weaknesses rather than identifying your personal issues. It creates animosity when constantly shortcomings are pinpointed in a negative manner. Perfect marriages do not exist, but relationships constantly grow and evolve over time. They must be nurtured and kept alive by being attentive to the needs of your partner. Do not let your marriage die due to boredom and complacency. Your plan does not have to be complexed, for example, if your mate complains you are not a good listener. That is an easy fix; simply remove all distractions and give them your undivided attention. Your response to their comments indicates whether you are truly listening to their concerns. It may be simple to you, but extremely important to your mate. When your behavior has been modified, it will be noticed and can lead to new possibilities to build a better relationship. Do not be afraid to change or try a different approach. Just ask yourself, "Has the current situation continued to remain the same?" If so, then be innovative and try a different approach. Try to identify their criticism of your behavior and create an improvement plan. This approach will de-escalate conflict and tension and allow the relationship to reset and start afresh.

Quality Time

Relationships built to last constantly require restoration like an old antique. An update to improve its appearance so marriage is a lifetime investment that requires close attention. It is a lifetime commitment, and it requires expressions of passion, intimacy, and quality time. Life is too short just to have a great résumé of accomplishments. At the end of the day, you are at the top of the ladder in your career and in the cellar with your marriage. To cultivate your marriage plan to spend quality time together. Quality time does not just include a vacation once a year, it is enjoying the simple things, watching a movie together, or doing things as a couple. The common thread with those who divorce is they simply grew apart. It amazing how many couples live in the same home in different rooms function publicly as a couple but live like strangers. If you love your mate, create an environment where they do not have to compete for your attention. Ensure your life is inclusive of quality-time events which will foster your relationship. It is amazing how couples can love their pets, caress them, and display so much affection, but their bedroom is colder than an Arctic iceberg. Do not allow your marriage to stagnate. Use the same approach when you captivated each other's hearts and create an atmosphere of romance. Marriage is a lifetime investment; if you take care of it, will pay lasting dividends.

My wife and I have been married for over 40 years, and she is still the love of my life. We have experienced many trials and tribulations just like any other couple had our differences, but our commitment has remained intact. I attribute this to our faith and true love which can endure anything if two people are willing to compromise, communicate, forgive and foster excitement in their relationship.

Chapter 7: Caretaker's Commitment for Care

Providing care for family members who are terminally ill or suffer from a debilitating condition creates an array of emotions which are difficult to manage. I tried to cover up my emotions and provide care for my father who was terminally ill with prostate cancer. He served in the army and had a strong work ethic. In addition, he enjoyed the outdoors, hunting, fishing, raising farm animals, and gardening. He trained me in many aspects of life including being a handyman, mechanic, and how to care for animals. I realize as an adult many of the lessons helped me develop into the person I am today. I never understood why in many ways he appeared hard on me as a child as compared to fathers of other children in the neighborhood. My day consisted of chores in the garden, feeding animals, and working at the house, from mowing to painting. Now I understand why I have a strong work ethic and a good knowledge of agriculture. I have a green thumb due to him empowering me with the knowledge of how to cultivate a garden. In addition, as a child, I did not understand why it was important to learn how to change automobile parts when I did not even own one. Now I have the knowledge to perform minor maintenance on vehicles and insight regarding repairs. Due to him I acquired many skills which are cost-savers and skills I can impart to my children. He layered me with knowledge like paint in different layers, so I would be prepared for the future and could draw back from all the things I was taught as a young man. I still recall how to perform so many things during my youth which appeared a waste of time but now realize these skills' true value. Each task I was taught was a new layer of knowledge in so many areas. It is important as a parent we teach our siblings the basics because this knowledge will last a lifetime.

He was an immensely proud man who worked hard to make provisions for his family. Just like anyone in life, he had his strengths and weaknesses.

Due to the way I was raised, he instilled in me the desire to work hard to accomplish my goals. I acquired many useful skills from his guidance that help me today. Due to him, I was motivated to learn and take advantage of the opportunities that life presented me. He often stated a man who does not work will not eat.

My father was a strong, independent man who worked his entire life. No one gave him anything, but he labored to build his own home in a country setting. He and my mother had 3 children, of whom I was the youngest sibling. They provided care for their family until we all reached the age of maturity and left home. As time passed, my parents divorced and my father lived alone. He retired from his job after over 30 years to enjoy his life.

He was diagnosed with prostatic cancer around the age of 62 and had surgery to remove the tumor. Later he was diagnosed cancer-free. It was around his early 70s when the cancer returned. This man was physically fit, who at one point weighed upwards of 230 pounds, living alone caring for himself after his retirement. As time progressed, he slowly began to lose the ability to care for himself and required someone to assist him. He lost his ability to drive and walk. One day he could physically feel the tumors in his body. His health deteriorated and he required assistance with feeding, bathing, and getting into the bed. His weight diminished to a little over 100 pounds. During this time, I put on my best face to appear strong, passionate, and understanding. He made frequent visits to the doctor due to the loss of blood in his body which affected his heart rate. Once he received a blood transfusion, he would improve, but the visits to the doctor became more frequent. His doctor requested all the family members to accompany him on his next visit. He stated his condition was terminal and referred him to hospice care. My father decided to have hospice care provided at his home.

According to an article in Wesley Life, 1.8 million people enter into hospice care, 66% receive care at home, and 27.4% receive care at inpatient care facility (Wesley Life, 2014).

It was a difficult time for me to watch him literally fade away before my eyes. Again, you paint your face with the appearance of support and strength to encourage your loved one in a good emotional place. Once a strong man an image of strength slowly faded from independence to total dependence of care. As the saying goes if you live long enough, you may experience being once a man and twice a child. This simply implies you were born a child requiring care, and due to age or sickness, you end up requiring similar assistance. As a caregiver just assist and you show love. Each day you attempt to focus on the positive things in life by reminiscing upon the past. You put on the right appearance of strength but inside, you hurt and hold back the tears. Although you know the outcome, it does not help you understand the pain, while someone you love suffers and will eventually transition to the afterlife.

Acceptance

This process of assisting someone with a terminal condition requires acceptance of their fate and inner strength to endure what will soon occur. Emotionally again during each visit your paint yourself as a pillar of strength to encourage your loved one. Those who truly know you can look beyond the disguise and see your discomfort. Always putting on the superhuman facade and attempting to be an encourager when deep down you are hurting as well. You cling to your faith to motivate yourself and speak positive things in their presence to encourage them. Mentally you ponder the thought one day they will be relieved from their pain. This fresh pain flows through your mind every time you think about the reality of what is to come. To be in control of your emotions, it requires acceptance of God's will. The other amazing fact was even though my father was terminal, he had faith that death was not the end. He believed in the afterlife and death could not separate him from his destiny. He had accepted Jesus Christ as his personal savior and was not worried about death. My father also realized his life was ending. He prepared all his children for his imminent death.

Emotional Release

During this experience, my emotions were up and down. Some days, I was so positive and other days I needed someone to encourage me. Life is full of new adventures, about discovering who we really are on the inside. It is during these difficult times you learn a lot of things about yourself. You develop an inner strength to be a person who can release your emotions and rise to the occasion to help a loved one depart in peace. You can overrule your emotions and find peace in showing love. How can you find peace and strength to endure this situation? Some say pray all the time or seek out your friends to keep you in a safe place. Well, to be honest, when you are emotionally full, sometimes you will cry in despair. Crying is not an admission of defeat or being out of control, but a way for your body and mind to release stress. When this happens, just realize you are human and there is a limit to what you can bear. After the release, renew your mind with meditation. Your loved one really needs you during this difficult time and is fully aware of the impact their suffering has upon their loved ones. It is important to reassure them that everything will be fine and just as they have accepted their fate, they can not let go and be in peace without your support. It will require meditation and focus on your behalf to embrace the mind-set of controlling your emotions. This is a time when the family must lay aside all personal conflicts and display unity in the family. The pain is always fresh during the last days of a loved one's life.

Reassurance

No one desires to see their loved one suffer, especially when no cure is available. It is difficult to observe them when their health is failing. I can remember times being caught between going to visit your loved one or just staying away. You feel condemned when you do not visit and fresh pain while you visit. Love is a powerful medication which will give you the strength to perform duties necessary to provide care. It will also provide emotional comfort when you are doing the right thing. Reassurance is required for you as a caretaker to endure this season of suffering. In addition, your loved one requires reassurance to let go. They are entering the final phase of their lives and are preparing to depart into uncharted territory. Terminally ill patients will go through several phases such as denial, depression, and finally acceptance. It is important during this time for you to access all the support and guidance available to help you be prepared for what is about to happen. There are many resources available through ministers, hospice and grief counselors, or group therapy. Your loved one during this time needs the assurance from you that life with continue in a positive way upon their demise. Reassure them with confidence that the family will continue to work together and remain strong.

The Last Days

During the last days of life for our loved one is the most difficult time. My father in his last days slipped into a coma. One thing to remember, they can hear your conversation, but many times are too weak to respond. I continued to talk to my father while he was in a coma. I will never forget after he had been in a coma for three days and was unresponsive, something miraculous occurred. I started singing my favorite song to my father *Blessed*

Assurance. Immediately after I finished the song, he began to hum the song verbatim even though he was so weak and could not speak. This was his way of letting me know he was able to hear me and was ready to depart. He passed on that same day. My father had an expression of peace upon his face to reflect to the world he was in a good, spiritual place.

The comfort I had making his arrangements was with the satisfaction that I was there when he needed me the most. I had done my best as his son to help him through his transition. I do not have difficulty when I visit his resting place because I gave my all. A loved one must understand their limits and afterward be able to release their emotions to have peace. It is important in those last days to help them transition because the benefits are reciprocal for the caretaker and your loved one. These last days can be like riding on a roller coaster, but understand, when a person departs in peace, they are free from the cares of this world. The last days are a celebration of life and their contributions to their family. Our loved ones will live forever in our memory. They leave a legacy of laughter, precious moments, and lessons learned. These memories and learning points are designed to help us continue life and pass them on to the next generation. We grieve but not to despair because their legacy continues to live through their descendants.

(Story) Encouragement to Let Go

I had a great friend who provided so much love and support for others throughout his life. He displayed a passion for helping the youth, and they embraced his love with uttermost respect. For over 45 years, he served in the role of helping the youth better their lives. His journey was being a father to the youth who did not have a male role model in their lives. He was hospitalized due to a stroke which impacted his ability to speak. A few weeks later he had another stroke and was in a coma. Due to his condition he was transferred to hospice for care. Immediately I went to visit him at hospice, and he was alone in the room. I grabbed his hand and prayed with a reminder of how he influenced so many lives. Due to his love for others, many youths without a clear future through his stewardship had a path for success. The greatest fear of most people is to be alone. I reassured him of his faith, and he was not alone, and it was acceptable to release his life. My last words were to encourage him for a job well done. He had done well, and it was time to rest. A couple days later he transitioned to the afterlife.

Caretaker for Mentally Disabled

It is difficult to imagine how you can lose a person you love who is still alive. This is the scenario of what happens when you are a caretaker for a loved one who slowly loses their mental capacity over a period of time. NAMI.org estimates that 1 in 5 adults in the United States experience mental illness—43.8 million each year, and 1 in 25 experience serious mental illness—11.4 million each year.

(Story) My Mother's Journey

My mother was a beautiful person who loved her children and family. A person full of life who cared for her family and made her home a place of peace. She instilled strength, integrity, and a strong work ethic from our youth to adulthood. A mother's love is almost indescribable simply because they are willing to sacrifice everything to provide for their children. This wonderful lady whom I loved with a passion, in my eyes, was just the perfect mother. She was always there when I needed her the most, providing encouragement, advice, discipline, and enduring love. Life was good from a young child until adulthood. I remember departing at 18 years of age to serve in the United States Air Force. She was there waving with my father as I began a new career. They both poured into my life all they had to help me succeed. I returned about 4 years later to my family in Texas to a mother with open arms and a wonderful smile. My mother was gainfully employed and was divorced. Our family life was happy, and everything appeared to be moving in the right direction.

One day she felt bad and was unable to return to work. I just felt it was a temporary situation, but it continued to the point she just quit her job. My mother just stated she was sick and unable to work without any doctor visits or diagnosis. This was a shock, and no one really understood why she would suddenly resign from her job and not even give proper notice. I accepted her explanation and began to transition from military to civilian life by securing employment. I did what a good son would do and provide for his mother. As time progressed things began to change about her, such as being paranoid and feeling someone was out to do her harm. A tragic situation occurred in our family which just pushed her further away from reality. Her mental capacity diminished quickly, and she became a danger to herself and others. During this time, she required professional guidance that diagnosed her condition as paranoid schizophrenic. For her to receive proper treatment, it had to be court-ordered; therefore, I had to go through the judicial system to commit her to a mental health hospital. This was the beginning of a journey that lasted over 30 years. My mother would require support and care for the rest of her life. I later married and was called into the ministry and became a pastor. It was through my faith and prayers, the Lord provided me strength to endure this difficult trial. Throughout these years, it was episodes of her having mental occurrences which required constant treatment. Her life evolved from the point where she could function in assisted living to the point where she required full-time care. My sister and our family were the primary caretakers until she transitioned to the afterlife at the age of 87.

It is difficult to describe how this experience can impact you emotionally to observe someone you love slowly lose their mental capacity to function. As a caretaker, it is difficult to care for anyone who is seriously ill, but when it is a mental issue, it is different. During regular visits, conversations may start out being normal but end up with comments that are not logical. You attempt to understand and accept the nature of their condition, but it is painful to observe a loved one who is alive, but their mental capacity has diminished. The emotional duty of the caretaker is to provide the best care possible. It was heart-wrenching to remember my mother the way she was and face this new person who appears to be the same but acts differently. Year after year it was a cycle of care for my mother with mental breakdowns throughout the years.

Acceptance of the Condition

To help my mother, I had to first accept her condition and the responsibility for her care. It would require a tremendous amount of emotional energy to provide the care necessary to assist her along with the demands of my own family and ministry. No matter how strong you may be, it requires prayers to remain focused. It was not an easy task to undertake. To perform long-term care, you cannot personalize the situation. Just remain focused on the task at hand. If you allow your emotions to dictate your life, it will take you to a place of despair.

No matter how much help someone requires, please remember to maintain your physical and mental health. You can set yourself up for failure by denying your personal life and maintaining your family structure. Denying yourself personal time or discontinuing your life will slowly drain your energy required to maintain a balanced life. Despite whatever is going on in your life, a spiritual fight continues for inner peace. Remember anytime you totally dedicate your life to something, other areas will lack. The demand for your help will always be required; however, you must develop the boundaries to ensure your family life is balanced. This advice is necessary to balance the heart-felt tendency and desire to satisfy your loved ones. It is the right thing to do; however, not at the cost of straining another relationship with a spouse or children. The only person who really understands how to make you happy is you. Do not give up on life nor discontinue doing things you enjoy. Accept the condition and develop a balanced plan to include this situation and continue your life. Yes, this includes quality time dedicated for yourself.

Family Effort

This was a difficult situation and a lifetime commitment, and no one person can provide all the care; it requires family members working together. It is important to have family support, whereby each member can assume certain roles to help. In my situation I had a loving wife and sister to assist and encourage me through this journey. My sister was a faithful caregiver to my mother. In addition, my mother had siblings and a host of others throughout her life who would check on her to provide support. I also say some family members cannot bear the emotional requirement to provide care to a loved one. You can judge them and expect more but they simply cannot bear the pain. Learn to accept what they offer but continue to encourage them to offer more. This can be also a time of turmoil, blame game, and meltdown. During this period, a family must reach above their own feelings and develop a plan of care and support for their loved one. All families have a history consisting of good and bad situations that were divisive. What I have noticed is there is always one who will rise to the occasion and be willing to make the ultimate sacrifice to ensure things are done properly. This person may embrace the lion's share of responsibility to ensure their loved one receives the proper care. Families will not always agree on medical decisions asset distribution, but they can foster love in unity and support their family members in care.

Chapter 8: Caring for the Special Needs

Every parent is excited to welcome a wonderful new baby child to the family. The mother at birth is just praying for a healthy child. Newborn babies are the picture of innocence and add value to the family. The proud father and a mother are ecstatic with their first child and simply look forward to holding it in their arms. Many children are born with defects that are recognized immediately while others are discovered as they grow and develop. As a parent of a special-needs child, I know the impact it has upon the family structure. The responsibility for care can be extremely demanding even if the care is provided by the parent or in a care facility. This journey requires patience, prayers, and self-encouragement. Many parents who provide care to children with disabilities must be the advocate with their physician, attend counseling sessions, and learn how to provide special care. The responsibility since the discovery of the condition creates a variety of emotions to deal with a lifetime of care. This journey for the parents is a lifetime commitment.

The Big Decision

The big decision involves how the care will be provided whether in home or perhaps group home. Many factors come into play such as financial aspect, lifestyle change, commitment to lifetime care, and emotional impact on the family. If the family consists of a two-parent family, both must be involved in providing the long-term care plan. Decisions should be agreed upon, especially in a marriage. Just consider the emotional impact on the family's ability to cope with just having a differently abled person in the home. I remember visiting a group home and noticed a beautiful little girl with a lovely smile who had physical and mental challenges. The staff mentioned the parents placed her in care when she was an infant and never returned for a visit at the group home. They further explained the father was a medical doctor and the mother could not emotionally accept the fact their daughter was differently abled. Due to the stress upon the mother, they decided to place the child in group care and provide the necessary financial support. These types of situations occur due to parents not being able to deal with the stress created by their differently abled child. In other situations, I have seen mothers fully dedicate their lives to caring for their child and ensuring they are just another member of the family. The first decision is who and how will care be provided.

Long-Term Care

One of the most difficult situations when a child is differently abled requires a decision what type of long-term care is best. There are emotional ramifications with all decisions. A parent must decide what is best for their situation. Every parent has a special love for their child, and the most difficult decision is to place their child in a group home. The decision to keep them at home with the demands on long-term care is also a life-changing event. Depending on the level of their disability, many of these children require full-time care. They require assistance with eating, clothing, and bathing. In addition, many are not able to communicate verbally but can learn to in other ways. It also becomes an issue when a parent with a child who needs care, but the family cannot financially make this commitment to provide full-time care. This decision involves other family members in the household. The alternative is to place them into full-time care. Once they are placed into care, it requires establishing a plan to create a family life of activities. You are committed to raising a child who does not reside with you. These children will require therapy and sometimes corrective surgery, and in addition, clothing and other necessary things under your care. I have seen many parents emotionally struggle simply because of the pain of not being able to provide the proper care at their homes. In many situations it is obvious from the beginning that as the child grows, the parents are not physically able to provide the child with care. In addition, some family members cannot bear the emotional energy required to develop relationships. They accept the reality of the situation and simply try to do their best. We must remember these children did not choose their condition. It is difficult to understand why children are born differently abled, but it is a fact of life. They are human beings who are functional at certain levels and still able to share and feel love. One of the misconceptions of the differently abled is to assume they are without human understanding. However, they are smart and capable of communicating their desires even with a less-than-perfect physical ability. When these children are taken to public events or restaurants, many individuals stare and take notice of the fact that they are different. Just remember a disability does not have to be from birth but can be caused by accidents or sudden illness. The caregiver has the responsibility of loving a child who many will not take the time to understand or build a lasting relationship.

It is amazing when those with special needs interact in group activities such as luncheons and recreational activities. They communicate among themselves and most love to dance and enjoy good food. Sounds like something that most people enjoy.

Our Daughter's Love Story

Our differently abled daughter was born with several conditions which has limited her ability to function as others. One of her challenges is the ability to speak a clear language although her comprehension is excellent. Due to her condition it has required full time care since birth. She is almost 38 years old with beautiful eyes and a wonderful smile. Just like any other person once you get to know them hidden charming attributes are discovered. Just to think about our experiences with her causes laughter especially how she comprehends and expresses her emotions. Our daughter enjoys good music and loves to dance. It is during the annual Crystal Ball when all her friends who are differently disabled dress up in formal attire and really let their hair down. Her group of friends really know how to dance the night away. They come to this event with dates or as a group and despite all their physical and mental challenges dance across the floor. Just like anyone else they express the same emotions displaying the latest dance moves. Her favorite food is chocolate especially after a good meal. I anxiously wait for a particular expression when her meal is complete, and she gives me that look. It is time for dessert. She cannot verbally express herself but is a master at utilizing body movements to communicate her concerns. When she just wants attention, she will grab your hand and hold it or place it around her neck. She celebrates all the holiday season with her siblings. One of her favorite past times is to just cruise down the street while listening to music. When dressed in a new attire she is fully aware and makes it known she is looking good. During our excursions out in public many people just stare but we just hold hands and walk in the restaurant and enjoy our meal. Sounds like what any person would enjoy.

Although these comments sound like a breeze she requires a tremendous amount of care. She has experienced medical episodes throughout her life but continues to smile. The best way to know what she desires is by spending quality time with her. This will improve better methods of communication. Her mother is a hero and the best caregiver anyone could ask for to provide care and support. I have experienced the joy and pain with my wife over the years and often encourage her through difficult times. A mother's love runs deep for she cares for all her children and carries their burdens. We both have endured the joy and pain of being a caregiver. Our daughter has only spoken two words consistently her entire life Daddy and Momma. This lets us know she understands our love is heartfelt. Our daughter has been an integral part of our family because we chose to make it a priority.

Caregiver

The Commitment I applaud caregivers who make the decision to provide full-time care in their homes. It is important to understand no parent desires to see their child in a differently abled status. It is painful to see them suffer with conditions that sometimes will not improve but grow worse over time. It takes courage to rise above your pain to do the right thing and ensure joyful events are planned throughout their lives. This responsibility sometimes is a lonely one because many others simply do not care or perhaps cannot handle the emotional suffering. The caregivers must be ready for emergency hospital visits or accidents and ensure proper care has been provided to their child. This lifetime commitment from raising a differently abled child through adulthood requires the caregiver to provide care along with all other duties in their home. It is not an easy venture but only by rising above their mental and emotional pain can this be done. This task even from infancy depending upon their mental and physical condition may require extensive care.

A Mother's Love

I provided encouragement to a mother who had raised her son since infancy. A perfect mother providing care without hesitation, sacrificing her life to raise her differently abled son. It was easy to bath feed and clothe him when he was small. It was busy work but fun and his condition was not overwhelming. When her son grew into an adult, his aggressive behavior and her age became a factor. Just like any mother she had deep affection for him, but she realized his care required a new direction. It was a fact due to her age and limited physical abilities, she would not be able to provide sufficient care for him. His physical strength overpowered her small frame. She had to decide to place him into a group home for his care. Due to her maternal instinct, it caused her great pain to let him go. She had episodes of depression and crying in despair. I reassured her that providing for his long-term care was the best decision. Once he was placed into a group home, he adjusted to the change. A mother's love always desires to hold her children close and provide them care. Although it was a good decision, she had to live with the reality her son was not with her. She reconnected with her faith to learn one thing—her son was in the best place. If something happened to her, she would know he was well adjusted and receive proper long-term care. These decisions are difficult and are not made without emotional pain.

Parents develop close relationships with their child and learn to communicate in different ways so they can fully understand their needs. The entire family is impacted by the demand upon the caregiver to provide loving care and maintain their daily family activities. This may also affect the other siblings in the household who require quality time to bond as well.

Just a simple visit to the grocery store or a doctor visit can result into major challenges. The public often subjects the special-needs' population to stares and acts of curiosity. During public outings, many onlookers do not understand being different is not a bad thing. Many individuals have disabilities that are not noticeable, while others are obvious. Just because a person does not act the normal way, somehow, they are not without feelings. In addition, many in the medical field struggle with treating those with disabilities.

Social Acceptance

The frustration of a caregiver for the differently abled impacts them regardless of their socioeconomic backgrounds. The fact is many people do not understand how to develop relationships with the differently abled. They are accustomed in their circles to having individuals with cognitive skills but not those who are mentally challenged. Due to the lack of disability awareness, they are unaware some of the greatest minds reside in those with a disability. It is an untapped source of opportunity for great contributions to our society. They provide valuable resources in the employment sector by working in areas of their abilities. Due to the physical limitations many may overlook their mental capacity. Employment opportunities should be based on their ability to perform the essential duties of the job. Individuals with disabilities are limited in one area by a physical/mental condition but still have skills to perform many functions in the job. In fact, based upon my experience, they excel at certain jobs and exhibit soft skills which many employers are seeking. The focus on these individuals should not be on their limitations but on their abilities and skill set. Those who are differently abled, many times, must overcome bias and negative perceptions to find employment. I have witnessed individuals with a variety of disabilities with the aid of a job coach and training provide employers with a productive workforce.

Becoming Differently Abled

In addition, many simply do not understand how easy it is to become differently abled due to accidents or a sudden medical condition. Life is unpredictable and without notice our lives can change instantly due to a tragedy or major illness. These events impact the family financial structure and housing arrangements and create a new responsibility in the household. A person who becomes differently abled experiences life-changing events. Life has changed from what they once were able to accomplish adjusting to new limitations caused by their disability. The mental and physical impact to a life-changing event requires family support and someone must become a caregiver. The caregivers deal with the responsibility of care and many frustrations in our society.

Another area of concern involves the family and relatives' interaction with those with disabilities. Due to a person's disability, their interaction and conduct may be unusual with most but normal with those who understand their behavior pattern. This perception can create tension simply because of the lack of social acceptance. The truth of the matter is they have a right to be treated with dignity and respect. It is the caregiver who perceives and feels the pain due to others' reactions and lack of concern. Life does not end with a disability, but alters the way life will be conducted in the future. The person who is differently abled endures much frustration and pain, especially going from once being able to care for themselves to the point of requiring assistance to perform simple tasks. Family support is paramount to promote hope and encouragement to our loved ones.

Acceptance

There are two areas of acceptance—one being the person is differently abled and second their family is accepting the required responsibility. Full acceptance is the realization that life has changed and a new destiny with challenges is in the future. It will take mental, physical, and spiritual strength to overcome these new obstacles.

Let us use our imagination you were suddenly differently abled, confined to a wheelchair, and unable to speak. Your voice has been limited to unintelligible sounds and the only way to communicate was through sign languages. Just a few questions: Would you still enjoy pizza, going to movies, shopping, fishing, or visiting friends? Consider even with these limitations, you enjoy going to your favorite restaurant and desire a sense of normalcy. This is what every person with a disability desires, simply to live and blend in with society and their disability be accepted as normal. This applies to life from public school through college and into the workforce. Acceptance is what the caregiver desires from family members and society. If you have a family member who is providing care for a differently abled person, they need your support. They love family and it is important for their life to be filled with love and a wholesome atmosphere. These individuals have a place in our society and deserve to have reasonable accommodations in all public facilities. Our society should have physical accommodations for recreational activities which sends a strong message to how we believe. All people are created equal with rights to have access to universal services for everyone.

Chapter 9: Losing the Love of Your Life

One of the greatest pain any person can endure is the loss of a spouse, child, or parent. Many times, others feel the grief process should be brought under control within a specific time frame. Every person deals with grief differently. In my pastoral experience, I have counseled and encouraged so many who grieved for years on their loved one's birthday. The memory of their loved ones continues to resonate in their mind and produces grief just like it was yesterday. The grieving process is normal for anyone who has suffered a great loss. It is important to understand even with this traumatic loss, the memory of your loved one will continue to exist. It is often during reflections at family occasions when the memories of a loved one will bring a smile and sometimes tears. Since everyone will suffer a loss during their lifetime, we must understand these feelings of loss are real. It is a process to overcome the emotional impact.

(Story) Lost with No Warning

Our suffering is often made fresh by the memory of a loved one which can be brought to bear by pictures, home movies, or just you reminiscing on previous memories. I recently lost one of my favorite nieces at the age of 40 due to a sudden illness. She was the only child, a beautiful loving person with a smile that would light up a room. I had been a part of her life since she was about five years old. We shared all the major holidays as a family, and she was just two years younger than my daughter. They were just like sisters throughout their life and shared many memorable experiences from elementary through high school. My niece married, and the couple joined my church. This couple's number-one prayer request was to have a child. They often stood together requesting prayerfully for this miracle to occur.

The answer to their prayers came and they had a son who was premature and required intensive care. This young infant was not fully developed, and there was great concern over his ability to overcome his medical condition. I received a call that his health was deteriorating, and he was being transferred to a regional hospital in the metroplex. Upon my arrival, I was made aware their young son who they prayed for had passed away. We were in the waiting room while they brought their deceased son into the family room. It was a visionary moment and I cannot forget the way she held her son. Her husband was heartbroken and speechless. This was devastating; after praying for years for the birth of their child, he was taken away so soon. Our lives are full of moments when loved ones are transitioned from this present life due to death. My beautiful niece was devastated but held on to her faith.

A few years later she attempted to have another child and birthed a beautiful baby girl who was healthy and full of life. This brought so much excitement to the family and it reassured their faith. In addition, as time passed, she birthed a son who was full of life and energy. Life seemed to be a bliss as the Thanksgiving holidays were full of laughter and these two little darlings sharing dinner with my family. My niece seemed to have the time of her life taking pictures, laughing, and enjoying the moment. At the end of the day another holiday had passed with great joy. We would start preparing for the Christmas holiday with great expectation of a fun-filled day.

My wife received an early-morning call from my daughter stating our niece had collapsed and went into cardiac arrest at her home. The ambulance had arrived, and she was taken to the hospital. She was a beautiful 40-year old married woman with a husband and two small children. I still hear and feel the desperation my wife had in her voice reflecting on what had happened. As I arrived at the hospital, family members were instructed to go into a waiting area, and I was told a chaplain would visit us. I knew based upon prior experience the outcome was her demise. I prepared myself to care for several of the family members when the physician stated they could not save her. Immediately the family was hysterical, and grief filled the room, but God gave us spiritual strength. I was able to comfort the family to the best of my ability. In order to be a vessel of strength, I did not shed tears but internalized my grief. I tried to be a voice of hope to all my family. They had more questions than answers. Her small children were in the waiting area bewildered and did not comprehend what just occurred. I continued to encourage this family including my own wife and children who were more like siblings to her than cousins. My source of strength was divine because inside I could still feel the fresh pain but did not allow it to overshadow my desire to console my family members.

It was due to a strong family bond which caused us to strengthen each other during this time of sorrow. Grieving alone with family support allows a family to begin the healing and acceptance process necessary to move forward in life.

Memory Flash

It was several months later when I called her mother at what I thought was a new number. I had an experience which occurred like none other. I was unaware she used her daughter's cell phone. When I called, she did not answer so it went to her voicemail. The voice was that of my niece with energy and tender, loving care. Just after being the pillar of strength for others for a long period of time, when I heard her voice, something just went through me like fresh pain. I had all the faith in the world, but her voice reminded me of the love I had for this woman. Her voice brought a fresh pain of her loss into my life that was real, just like it occurred yesterday.

Due to my emotional state, tears began to roll down my cheek. I called my wife and she could hear the discomfort in my voice and inquired what was wrong. With great sorrow I explained what occurred and how my grief had been suppressed until I heard her voice. My wife began to say words of encouragement to help me overcome my grief. I understand the loss of someone dear can be triggered by memories. The road to recovery starts with accepting your grief and appreciating all their wonderful memories. My niece made great contributions to our family and her life and memories continue to be celebrated. We all know the finality of death and once it occurs there is no return. It is important to learn how to cope with a loss and put value back into our lives. Memory flashbacks will occur often and sometimes seem mystical and more than a circumstance. We celebrated my niece's husband's and her child's birthday at a local restaurant and each time the server had the same name spelled the same way as our niece. We also celebrated her daughter's birthday with a large family gathering and her mother who kept her daughter's phone somehow called my wife just before we started to sing our happy birthday song. It is odd how things said or just occurrences often remind us of the loved ones we have lost. It is like they are still alive through our memory, and little reminders let us know they still are alive. Treasure those wonderful memories and do not allow sorrow to control your life. Learn how to smile when these memories flash as a reminder of the true love you shared. Celebrate their lives and appreciate the laughter because their memories will forever live in your mind. Although bad things may have occurred, focus on the good things and make them bittersweet. It is also important to encourage those who continue to grieve to overcome their feelings by focusing on the positive energy which our loved ones exemplified. It is important to redirect these mood swings and make their life a celebration. Choose words of comfort which uplift a person and paint a positive outlook rather than embracing their pain.

You have just endured a great loss, but recovery can be delayed due to mourning. Celebrate your loved one's life by renewing your mind-set to focus on the legacy they have left behind. Celebration includes a reflection on their great contributions and the fun moments. When David lost his son, he said, "I cannot bring him back, but I can go to him." Family members should celebrate during gathering when moments arise regarding departed loved ones to make it a joyful occasion. We can all still remember the famous quotes often recited by our parents. Their quotes left an imprint in our minds on how to handle adversity in our life. It is important to pass these quotes on to the next generation.

Time to Heal

It takes time to accept and mentally heal from a devastating loss. Family members will often worry whenever a loved one does not recover in a reasonable amount of time. They will get involved in your personal life with an attempt to help you feel better. Just as I stated, all people do not grieve the same way or recover as quickly as others. If the grieving process is not overtaken by hope and encouragement, it can completely consume a person's life. There are many options to dealing with grief, starting with professional counseling which can provide one-on-one assistance. Other options may include group therapy with others that experience the same condition. It is not always an easy process but will require effort to resist the desire to remain in a difficult mental state. It takes time to heal but you will never forget those you love. In addition, you must remove all guilt from your mind due to past broken relationships. It is easy to internalize your pain by blaming yourself for things that placed pressure on the relationship.

It may be true many situations were out of control and you desired things to be different while they were alive. It is impossible to change the past and therefore no action or feelings of remorse can go back in time to change what has already occurred. Just accept what occurred and move to a higher ground by expressing forgiveness for the painful memories in the past. Forgiveness starts with you accepting the things you cannot change but moving forward making each day a new day. Refuse to live in the past! Just like most of us, you could have done things differently. It is important at the right time to attempt to build back your normal life. If you are employed, it can be therapeutic in helping your mind focus on other things beside the fresh pain you have endured. Just return to normalcy which may include going back to work. Your work relationship with co-workers and interacting with them daily restores self-worth and redirects your focus. The mind is just like any other part of the body which when injured takes time to heal. It may seem hard to focus at first but continue to work and allow time to heal your pain. It is good to be able to discuss your true feelings because the only way to be free is to expose your fears buried in your subconscious mind. Allow your best friend or those who you really trust to provide insight into how you feel and share the negative thoughts that attack your mind. The healing process will be like a roller-coaster sometimes up and sometimes down. The worst thing to do is to deny your true feelings. Expose harmful thoughts that demean your character and rise to a new spiritual level by speaking positive things into your life. Do not allow other family members to draw you into negative situations or disputes resolve nothing but only raise everyone's anxiety level. Remember the human spirit is resilient against adversity. Live your life and enjoy all the benefits that each day brings.

Chapter 10: Loss of Innocence

Parenting is a lifetime challenge regardless of being single, married, or divorced. According to an article in Very Well Family, there are 13.6 million single parents who are responsible for raising 22.4 million children (Wolf, 2020). In addition, 80.4% are mothers and 19.6 percent are fathers. These single mothers are 40.6% divorce or separated and 42.6% have never been married. The family structure is important; however, a good parent can nurture their child to adulthood. We will discuss some of the issues children are facing in our society. It is our goal to provide insight and understanding how many children who evolve into adults have endured painful events. These layers of pain shape their character and outlook on life.

The most beautiful creation in the world is a beautiful newborn child. The first view is one of innocence as they lay in the maternity ward. It is simply an awesome view to observe them as they open their eyes to see the new world. They have left a place of protection where all their needs were being met inside their mother. This new child is a picture of innocence and naïveté and only seeks one thing—to be loved by their parents. Their joy comes from being held and hearing a gentle voice whispering words of comfort. This bundle of joy cannot speak but is full of feelings and can absorb the warm connection with their parents. It is this innocence that is adored and appreciation of life which brings joy to the mother and pride to the father. This beautiful baby is a new addition to the family, and the sex of the child is not important. The prayer is for a healthy child who can grow and develop without physical limitations. One of the most wonderful observations is caring for an infant as they develop so quickly from an infant to a toddler. It appears sometimes they just change and grow overnight. Children are totally dependent upon the care of an adult. It is the parent's responsibility to ensure their child's security plus provide for food and shelter. Their roles require constant care which is understood by parents and sometimes reluctantly accepted by the children. We paint the picture of family being a place of peace, tranquility, and love that is shared by all. It can be just that, but it also includes dysfunctional issues and abusive situations. Children naturally love their parents who have been a symbol of security and trust.

It is when abusive situations occur within the family that a picture of frustration and insecurity is painted. These abusive behaviors begin to infiltrate the family structure. They start to paint a picture in a child's life which will follow them and impact how they will deal with real-life situations. During my tenure providing pastoral counseling, one of the most painful experiences involved counseling adults who experienced abusive behavior during their childhood. Many adults attempt to coverup the bad experiences, but they often resurface in relationships and in their marriage. It is devastating to a child when the person who should protect them is the one that causes them mental and physical harm through their abuse.

When a child is a victim of mental abuse, it paints a picture of insecurity and low self-worth into the child's mind. This is a common area of frustration of many of the young children abused during their childhood. It is an issue that many family members are embarrassed about and try to bury the issue. Just looking from the child's perspective, they take the courage to report the abusive situation which occurred to a responsible person. The parent has the responsibility to provide safety to their children. The abuser should be exposed, punished, and treated for their behavior. It sends a destructive message to a child when an adult chooses to not believe the victim but attempts to bury the situation. Men and women who have suffered from sexual abuse in their lives will carry that memory into every future relationship. Regardless of the actions of adults, the victim must live with the fact that no one believes them, and this act destroys their innocence. One could say I do not know who to believe. It is important to understand they need support and assistance to help them cope with what occurred.

This child has choices as they grow into adulthood, but they paint over this experience to build a happy life. It is when they began to build long-lasting relationships with a partner when these past experiences are resurrected.

The emotional pain which has been suppressed comes alive when they fall in love and are unable to trust another person with their innermost feelings. Since in their childhood no one believed their story, or they accepted and buried what occurred. No action was taken to truly validate their abuse. Now they must lower their emotional guard and allow someone inside a place of buried pain that has been closed since the bad experience occurred. They struggle to trust and may often release their true pain on someone else. Their shame and guilt refuses to allow anyone to enter their inner being to know how they really feel. It can be implied that no one understands. It is difficult to understand until they know their story and how a person really feels.

According to the National Statistics on child abuse and neglect, nearly 700,000 children are abused in the United States annually. In addition, 75% suffer neglect, 17.2% physical abuse, and 8.4% sexual abuse; four out of five abusers are the victim's parent (National Statistics Child Abuse 2019).

True healing happens when a person can release their frustration and let go of the painful past. Sometimes a relationship has issues which occur without an identifiable source of the problem. The problem may not even be in the relationship but locked into the subconscious of a person who was violated in an abusive situation. This painful situation creates a deep distrust to allow anyone into their innermost feelings. It occurs when relationships develop, and one person cannot allow themselves to love completely due to their past abuse. A person can begin to overcome their dark, painful past when they truly understand what occurred was not their fault. They can rise above their past pain and build a new, brighter future. This person desires to trust and love completely but two things must occur for them to be free.

I know the question is how you can help a person who has been abused. A victim needs support because they were violated in a way that mentally impacts the way they see and feel about their life. A good friend will always reinforce what occurred in their past was not their fault. Assist them through the process of acceptance, survival, and restoration.

The first step is the acceptance of what occurred. Regardless of who caused the pain, whether by a stranger, friend, or relative, abuse did happen. The second step is to remove the factor of believability by not requiring anyone to accept their account of how or when the situation occurred. Seeking validation from others to believe their abuse without support will only accentuate their frustrations. The only voice that counts belong's to the victim. The third step is to understand it is not acceptable behavior for anyone to force their way upon anyone in an intimate manner. Many times, a person may attempt to block out the pain, but it will resurface until it has been removed by the acceptance of the truth. Although the abusive behavior did occur by another person, face it with a positive attitude. In addition, since it did not destroy them, they survived it. Reinforce tender loving care they should not allow their past to destroy their future. All human beings were wonderfully created and have a purpose in life. They are valuable, and their life brings a uniqueness to the world being they are one of a kind. The human spirit is resilient and can overcome even the most devastating circumstances. A survivor represents strength against adversity; if no one believes you, believe in yourself. Encourage yourself because what occurred was designed to destroy you. You are stronger than your past and you will not allow any prior abuse to impact your happiness. The best way to showcase your victory over an abuser is with success. Rise up, celebrate life, and do not allow your abusers rental space in your mind. Their punishment will be to observe your success and victory lap. It is your life; no one has the power to dictate your emotional state. Take away their power and live each day with joy and peace. This abusive experience was designed to leave a lasting negative imprint on the victim's life.

Accept the fact what occurred caused harm, but it did not destroy them. It is not your past which controls your future. Reject all the negative emotions and do not allow any form of condemnation to exist in your mind. What was designed to leave you broken and damaged will be your rallying cry for victory. Condition your mind to believe past experiences are stepping-stones for the future. Just like a glass of lemonade combines the bitterness of the lemon and the sweetness of sugar mixed with water to create a tangy refreshing taste. Develop a strong resistance to the memory which desires to take you to a dark place. Stand firm with acceptance and declare new liberties within your spirit. Do not allow past experiences to dictate your future. Control conversations with optimism and do not allow others to treat you as a helpless victim. Just as a substance abuser declares I have been sober for a certain period, you must declare and accept this painful situation occurred and live your life knowing better days are ahead.

Abusive Behaviors

Mental abuse can come in many forms including preferential treatment among family members. It can be insinuated one child has athletic or academic abilities, naturally drawing attention away from others who do not possess similar attributes. Playing favorites in a family is detrimental and forever exists in a person's memory even when they deal with adult issues. It is amazing how adults bring up the matter of their childhood about who was the favorite one or the black sheep. It is important to equally praise your children's success regardless of whether one exceeds the other. Set the tone of equality among children in the household. This does not mean to neglect to recognize the success for one child because of concern for another child. Children love attention and for their parents to praise them for their achievements. Teach your children to celebrate each family member's success.

Verbal abuse is another common form of abusive behavior which causes tremendous mental anguish. Words live for a lifetime in the minds of a child, whether positive or negative. We all have reprimanded our children for bad behavior which is right and necessary for their development. The stories being told by many incarcerated individuals is deeply related to some form of abuse in their childhood. What occurred in their early life does not justify the crime they have committed in the present, but it allows them to find a crutch to justify their actions. Many of the incarcerated young adults felt neglected by parents and sensed the parents' lack of concern for their future. I was providing encouragement to a person who was being sent away to prison for a long time; he, in our conversation, mentioned his family never supported him. He indicated while he was in high school, his parents never attended his sporting activities. Again, this does not justify the crime, but the mind-set points out a picture of his mentality. Children require quality time and parental support. If they do not receive parental guidance, they will be affected by peer pressure. Their peers may influence them to make bad decisions which carry dire consequences. Parental guidance and control are essential over their child from infancy until adulthood. The difficulty arises when control and guidance were never provided during childhood.

Once this child become a teenager without proper guidance, parents try to exercise control and face strong resistance.

During one of my counseling sessions with the parent of an out-of-control youth, she was living in fear and felt helpless. One mother stated she feared her son and he refused to respect her instructions. She simply gave up and let him rule the home. This young man did not contribute to the home by working or provided any assistance to his mother. The problems are created by not exercising control while these children are developing their behavior patterns. Parents must redirect their children's bad behavior when the children are in the development phase. If children are allowed to develop without guidance, as they become teenagers, they will be out of control. So, what are possible solutions? Authority must be exercised and demonstrated, and one of the common mistakes is trying to treat an adult just like a child. Verbal confrontations and threats from parents sometimes sound like a broken record to young adults. These tend to lose their effectiveness. One of the greatest tools of breaking down barriers is just listening without judgment and allowing a person to vent. The reason many youths develop a closer relationship with their peers is because their friends simply listen to their side of the story. The important thing a parent must understand is to discover the source of conflict, and this cannot occur without listening to gain insight. Regardless of whether their thoughts are childish or without merit, it is important their voice be heard. Sometimes parents forget some of their bad experiences during their youth and just become an authoritarian figure. A young adult needs a friend and a parent. A parent who can communicate with their child opens the door for them to release their concerns. The parent must be the decision-maker based upon what is best for their child. A possible solution offers a peace treaty and flips the switch to remove the anger and de-escalate the situation. Create an atmosphere where you both can be open about your feelings without leading to a verbal confrontation. Identify the source of the conflict and work toward solutions. Promote flexibility, but as a parent you must stand your ground on issues which are important. This process will create an atmosphere to improve your overall relationship.

Bullying

According to PACER National Bully Prevention Center, the National Center for Education Statistics indicates the incidence of female students experiencing bullying is 6% compared with that of male students at 4%. Bullying experiences occur at a rate of 43% at schools, 43% in classrooms, and 15% by form of text messages. In addition, 46% report incidents to an adult at school (National Center for Education Statistics, 2016).

As a young man in school, I was a victim of bullying by an older student who would threaten bodily harm to me daily. I was too embarrassed to tell anyone about my situation because I was growing into manhood and did not want to appear weak. I chose not to disclose this problem to my older brother or my parents. I allowed this fear to fester in me to appear cool among my friends. This senior's behavior occurred frequently at school every time I would encounter him. He would push me around and threaten bodily harm because of being older and larger to me in size. I have a clear understanding of how individuals who have been bullied feel emotionally. A bully is really an insecure person who is using what they perceive as an advantage to create fear in the hearts of their victims. The first problem I had was to overcome my fear of what others would think of me for exposing this person as a bully. This is the area where parents should spend time with their children when they are young and throughout adolescence to explain types of bullying tactics. Let them know first that admitting they are afraid is not a sign of weakness. Second, only when it has been exposed can the situation be resolved. I discussed what was happening to me with my best friend and we confronted the bully about their behavior, and it would cease immediately. The bully simply backed away and the behavior ceased. The importance of communication with your child is to make them aware bullying is not acceptable and must be addressed. Bullying is more common than you can believe, but it can be resolved without violence. Violence will send the wrong message and will have possible criminal repercussions. Teach and train your child about bullying and how to rectify it by exposing the perpetrator. It is not a sign of weakness but exercising power over their greatest weapon which is fear. Individuals not trained about these tactics are unaware about how to resolve their problems which can lead to certain decisions. It is important as a parent to not assume everything is well but routinely remind them how to handle a bully.

Where are my Parents?

The ideal household should consist of the mother and the father together raising their children. The mother and father have characteristics which help the child develop into maturity. It is a fact the number of single parents and grandparents raising children has increased significantly. I applaud those parents who despite spousal separation provide support and love for their children. They make a commitment despite a failed relationship to continue provide support for their child which is a lifetime duty. It simply is not out of an obligation but pure, devoted love and will not allow any circumstances to prevent them from having a significant role in their children's lives. The dedicated parents should be appreciated and made known they are impacting their children's life in a positive manner.

I am imparting my perspective from the view of children who are being raised without one of the parental figures in the family. This can occur due to birth out of wedlock or divorce. It is absolutely mind-boggling how children are affected by not having both parents and the emotional luggage they carry from childhood through adulthood. My intention is not to insinuate a parent is a deadbeat.

It is my purpose to bring to the forefront the child's perspective of not having a father or mother figure in their lives in these situations. The child born out of wedlock in many situations may not know their father or will have never met him. The difficulty arises when the child does not know why a parent who had the opportunity to be a part of their lives for whatever reason chose not to be involved. It is their perspective that some attempt has been made such as writing letters or visitation to indicate they desire to develop a relationship.

We all know in our society divorce and broken relationships occur and both parents feel it is necessary to be separated. The separation is justified and accepted but what impact does it have on the children. A small child sleeps one night and wakes up the next day to find one of their parents has left. Perhaps attempts are made to make them understand along with promises made which fade over time. It is the divisiveness of the relationship which often results in broken contact between a couple that fails to consider the lifetime emotional effect on their child.

Divorce and Impact on Children

According to an article in Focus in the Family, Wallersteins's (2000) study conducted from 1970 to 1990 followed a group of youth for 25 years after the divorce of their parents. These youth continued to have substantial expectations of failure, fear of loss, change, and conflict. Parents separate and move on, but the children carry this experience into adulthood, regardless of the cause of divorce a family has been separated. This child who once had both parents now only has one. They struggle with the divorce but deep down inside hold a glimmer of hope that one day the parents may reconcile. These children have passionate love for both of their parents even if one caused the divorce. They search for a reason and may not find one, but their anger and frustration are sometimes directed at the person who is providing care. This could possibly lead to behavioral issues and depression. A child's desires are simple, although they appear complex. They desire a relationship with both parents. In separations due to abusive situations, restrictions may be in place to protect them from the abusive parent; nevertheless, the children still have an emotional attachment with their parents. Our society labels people who abuse drugs or alcohol and have other issues as failures. These children still have one main desire that is to be loved and appreciated. Regardless of the anger, the bond which exists was created out of love. One parent focuses on their partner's faults, habits, and reckless behavior, but the children have a sense of a great loss. This void is only exacerbated when a loss of contact occurs over time caused by the separation. Children are more mature than most parents believe. Parents overcompensate for the lack of support of one parent, but children can see through broken promises. My point is simple: children suffer tremendously during a family separation and layers of painful memories exist within their subconscious throughout their lives. It is better for them to know their parents for who they are rather than being isolated. They can accept the fact all adults are not perfect parents. The major factor to them is not how well they measure up in society but how they relate to their children. It is important to understand but have a lot of questions and most of the time excluded from the true facts. It sometimes becomes such a bitter fight between couples about how and why things occurred they forget their children were created from the love they once shared.

It is crucial to have open understanding with your children so they will not build a fantasy relationship or allow anger to control their behavior. As a parent, recognize the signs. Take notice by observing their behavior and overall attitude changes as it pertains to activities they once enjoyed. A parent must take the time to ensure their child is in a good mental place. Develop lines of communication as it pertains to the children's thoughts and do not allow what occurred in the relationship to overshadow their desires for parental support. It is a hard job not to personalize a situation that has led to a divorce, but the children do not understand and need guidance through this process from both parents. Divorce is difficult, but do not allow it to continue to cause pain in the minds of the children. Parents simply should do the right thing for their children and communicate to help them process this separation. This will help the children not to internalize their pain and blame themselves with self-destructive behavior. Parents, children are crying out to say they need both of you in their lives. It is important to actively participate in their extracurricular activities and dedicate one-on-one time to provide a strong support structure. Also, I understand legal restraints may be in place in which children are prevented from visitation with their parent.

I Never Met My Father or Mother

It is good to know single parents raise their children and must assume the role of both mother and father. The fact is many children have never met either one of their biological parents or the simply been disowned as being their parent. This type of rejection from the children's perspective is a painful situation. They do not understand why their biological parent has not attempted to develop a relationship with them. The parent that has provided care attempts to provide whatever support they can extend, but the facts remains there is a desire to know more about the absentee parent. It is this rejection that turns to anger which surfaces during conversations about the identity and whereabouts of their biological parent. Once the child reaches adulthood, out of curiosity, sometimes, they will venture out to search and find their parent. Children again are a lot stronger than parents realize. Just being upfront about what is known about their biological parent prevents the blame from coming back to haunt you when they discover the truth.

Chapter 11: Suicide the Pain Left Behind

As a pastor one of the most difficult support roles is to assist a family who has lost a loved one due to suicide. It is a common fact many people throughout their lives had experiences which made them question whether life is worth living. It is obvious the person who committed suicide was in pain as well as the family that must continue to live with what occurred.

In my experience, many family members had no idea this person had suicidal tendencies. There are numerous religious and medical opinions about this matter. One thing is obvious they had problems which they could not solve, and death was an option with a high detrimental cost.

According to an article in Psychiatry Advisor, suicide is the tenth leading cause of death in the United States. In 2016, nearly 45,000 Americans died by suicide. Those left behind experienced guilt, blame, anger, grief, and depression (Yasgur, 2018).

Suicide victims have difficulty coping with stress which includes painful events including health concerns, financial burdens, tragedies, and sudden unresolvable crises. When people die by suicide, their family and friends often experience shock, anger, guilt, and depression

Key Factors That Lead to Suicidal Attempts

Stress

According to the CDC, every adult, teen, and even children experience stress. Stress comes in many forms, from financial issues, death, loss of a loved one, divorce, failure, broken relationships, medical issues, etc. Stress is a reaction to a situation wherein a person feels threatened or anxious without an obvious solution. The symptoms may be physical or emotional such as loss of appetite, increased appetite, isolation, and behavioral changes.

Professionals recommend that if problems persist or you are thinking about suicide, talk to a psychologist, social worker, or a professional counselor.

Helping Youth Cope with Stress

Children and adolescents often struggle with how to cope well with stress. Youth can be particularly overwhelmed when their stress is connected to a traumatic event—like a natural disaster (earthquakes, tornados, wildfires), family loss, school shootings, or community violence.

I have assisted families from all backgrounds who have lost a young person or a senior citizen who committed suicide. Also, I have provided pastoral counseling to individuals who have attempted suicide. My common theme has been "life is worth living."

(Story) The Will to Live

I provided support to a young middle-aged lady with several children. She was in a mental behavioral health hospital due to attempted suicide. This was her second attempt to end her life. It was difficult for her to overcome past failures and just desired to give up on life. Each time she would overdose on medications. During our counseling sessions she explained her pain would cause depression and overwhelm her emotionally. She had an overwhelming desire to end her life. This woman was religious but could not defeat her emotional pains. It was important to redirect her to believe life is worth living and to change her focus to positive energy. She found confidence in her faith to overcome her depressive mood swings. Along with professional help and prayers she began to grow and overcome her fears. She had to face her demons and make good decisions. Trials and tribulations do not have easy answers. This wonderful lady has been going strong for over ten years.

Death will occur in all our lives at its appointed time. We must all endure the struggles of life; no person in life can pick their trials and tribulations. It is not possible to wave a magic wand and expect life struggles to instantly dissipate. Life's struggles will test the human spirit's will and resolve to survive. Those who survive must fight with their complete mental and physical capacity to overcome adversity. It is not the trial or the failure which is the true test of human resolve but what occurs afterward. Does adversity cause a person to quit or to learn to grow and excel above their challenge? These truths do not say a person did not resist the desire to end their life because many factors are combined to lead to this attempt. The other issues may be clinical depression, drug abuse, and other factors which totally consumed a person's ability to overcome their condition. It is a difficult situation in which these attempts impact the innocent and other members of the family including children.

The Victim

According to CDC, the victim often plan their suicide attempt or it may be a spontaneous decision. These attempts are a cry of desperation and reaction to end their struggle. Friends and family members are left with a repetitive thought in their minds of, "If only I could have had five minutes to discuss their problems." These victims need information and support rather than judgment after the fact.

(Story) No One Knew His Pain

I remember a farmer who was a truly kind individual. He would always be isolated on side of the road talking to himself. One day he changed his behavior and took his wife out to eat and to an amusement park. She was so excited wondering what happened to her husband. During the middle of the night, she heard a popping sound which turned out to be a gunshot. Her husband had taken his life. We live in a society where so many are struggling to handle adversity, acceptance, and mental health. The victim's of suicide has a silent cry which is often not heard.

The Pain Left Behind

Any loss is painful, but the one caused by illness, accident, or natural causes allows their loved ones to accept it as being their time of departure. Suicide on the other hand takes away a person by their own actions which creates a layer of pain for their survivors. As stated by the CDC, one of the risk factors for suicide is a previous family member who perished by suicide. I have counseled family members of those who lost a family member due to suicide and their number one question is "why?" The family members who lost their father or a brother forever carry this pain of how they lost a special person and they were helpless to stop it from occurring. Although the victim has transitioned, this pain continues to live in the hearts and minds of those who loved this person. Due to the nature of death, some internalize the blame or rationalize in their minds what could they have done differently. They search for warning signs and try to understand how and what caused their loved one to commit suicide. The victim suffered and did not confide with anyone of their intentions, so no appropriate help could be provided. It is these moments which cause fresh pain. Suicide is difficult to understand because no one really has full knowledge of what the victim had experienced. The best way to deal with the pain is to understand whatever occurred was not anyone's fault. The victim had a stressful event which they could not resolve and decided to end their life. We do not have the power to change yesterday but must accept what has occurred, whether good or bad.

The first step is to not allow your conscious to fill your heart with guilt. Life is the most precious gift to mankind and therefore with time you can accept what has occurred was beyond your control. The loss hurts, but memories of the good times should be remembered.

Every person has an assignment with death; it is not easy when it was due to suicide. However, acceptance is the second step. It is important to know your limits and consider counseling to deal with the grief. Humans are the greatest pretenders of being simply fine when inside they carry a deep pain in a dark place. The process of healing is to expose how you really feel and allow this pain to be released.

It is a normal and good thing to do when grieving to find comfort by allowing someone to help you through this loss. The pain left behind is one of helplessness when others move from the mourning those who are close must live with the pain. There is no clear answer as to why it happened. It is important to know when you are facing a tragedy there is a higher source who can provide strength to those who are weak and hope in the hour of despair. Fresh pain is impossible to carry daily; it must be released. Take a deep breath and remember to love those who are around you. It is important to follow your heart when it tugs at you in the midnight hours to check on someone just to see if they are in a good place. It is hard to enjoy life carrying pain which deteriorates your joyful soul. Take away sorrow's power by loving those who are still in the land of the living. Invest your time and efforts to be available for family members. Depression is contagious and will impact others around you so be proactive to improve relationships with existing family members. Joy has the same affect, so be strong and refuse to lead a painful life full of defeat. Rise us and appreciate your life; begin this process one day at a time.

Chapter 12: Leading a Victorious Life

Life is full of events which impact a person emotionally throughout their lifetime. It is simply being able deal with diversity as it continually occurs. It sometimes feels like life is also a repeating cycle of events. These events bring up painful memories while others remind us of our victorious battles. It is not easy to write a script which magically solves all problems, while even the best advice may not provide positive results. It is important to know you were wonderfully made and created unique in a world of billions of people. The choice to be victorious requires action and faith to believe at the end of the day -better days are ahead. Our battles are won and lost daily. The battles we won are those in which we exercised our will to overcome defeat. The lost battles are the learning experiences that brought out vulnerabilities and identified the areas for improvement. Regardless of the cause of pain, whether from a broken relationship, divorce, loss of a loved one, or parental abandonment, it has caused emotional layers in our lives to overcome.

The most common suggestion from friends and family is just get over it and move on. That is advice provided with good intentions; however, all people are not the same and the time frame for recovery varies. If you are the person going through a difficult experience, just know the power already exists inside of you to be victorious. Simply stated, what was designed to defeat you caused significant pain, but it did not destroy the hero inside of you. There is a hero inside of every person designed to fight and overcome adversity. Sometimes the most difficult experience requires you to stand alone. Your spiritual mentality refuses to acknowledge defeat but responds aggressively with a plan to be victorious. This involves controlling what you think about yourself and the thoughts of condemnation from your own mind. The hero inside of you responds and acknowledges the truth of the pain but refuses to embrace it. The mind-set shifts from being a victim to being victorious.

Expose the Problem

One of the most important keys to overcoming a difficult experience is to expose how the situation caused you grief. Each period of tribulation has a lasting effect which is retained in your memory. It is impossible to forget life experiences; however, develop steps to manage your life which does not continue to keep you in a dark place. Refuse to internalize and hide a problem into a secret place which is detrimental to your emotional state. The power of freedom includes sharing how you really feel to someone who understands and provides sound advice. This is the first step toward recovery. It is not an admission of failure to seek help or guidance from different sources. When your situation has been shared with another person, you will realize many others have experienced the same emotional pain. Seeking a confidant, family or professional help, is significant because an objective opinion to your situation presents a logical approach to the matter. It prevents negativity and impulsive bad decisions which make matters worse. Exposure allows a release and relieves the pressure inside. It is difficult to carry around a painful experience and feel no one really understands. We have all made bad decisions and often we punish ourselves continuously without understanding the past cannot be undone. The feeling of being abused, being made a fool of, or being misunderstood is an experience which most can relate to. Exposing the problem makes a person release these anxieties. It is the egoistical approach when a person feels I can handle my business without help. The reason they cannot move forward is because they have not closed the door to past experiences. When an experience has closure, the pain subsides. Lastly is exhibiting positive energy about your life and its future. What was designed to defeat you emotionally and impact your future in a negative manner was met with positive energy. This energy was mobilized inside the human spirit to believe in oneself by faith that past experiences will not destroy the joy in one's soul. Remember to fight for your marriage and children. We lose our loved ones but their memories last for eternity.

Layers of Fresh Pain

In conclusion, your life consists of multiple layers of painful incidents and experiences. It is impossible to remove the layers because they are forever retained in your memory. The theme of fresh pain is acceptance and plants a banner in your soul you can survive and thrive. When you look at a beautiful antique which has several colors, only the outer color can be seen. It is only when you remove these layers to get down to the original color it is obvious all the history of the antique. No one can know all your colors unless you bring them to life. The important lesson is not to allow your life experiences to dictate your true color. You are bright, unique, and wonderful. Be victorious and an overcomer!

References

Birnbaum, G. E. (2018). The Fragile Spell of Desire: A Functional Perspective on Changes in Sexual Desire Across Relationship Development. *Personality and Social Psychology Review, 22*(2), 101–127. https://doi.org/10.1177/1088868317715350

Halberstadt, J. (2006). The Generality and Ultimate Origins of the Attractiveness of Prototypes. *Personality and Social Psychology Review, 10*(2), 166–183.

Little, A. C., Jones, B. C., & DeBruine, L. M. (2011). Facial attractiveness: evolutionary based research. Philosophical transactions of the Royal Society of London. Series B, *Biological sciences, 366*(1571), 1638–1659. Taken from: https://doi.org/10.1098/rstb.2010.0404

Grover, S., & Helliwell, J., 2019. "How's Life at Home? New Evidence on Marriage and the Set Point for Happiness," *Journal of Happiness Studies, vol 20*(2), pages 373-390.

National Center for Health Statistics, & Centers for Disease Control and Prevention. (2003) Marriage and divorce. Retrieved from Detailed marriage and divorce tables by state

https://www. cdc. Gov/nchs/fastats/marriage-divorce.htm

Crystal Raypole, Healthline, (2018 Why Do People Cheat in Relationships,

Retrieved from healthline.com/health/why-people-cheat

John B., Average Time Dating Before Marriage, (2020) weddingstat.org

https://www.weddingstats.org/average-time-dating-before-marriage/#:~:text=According%20to%20datingsiteresource. Com%20it,better%20before%20tying%20the%20knot.

Institute for Divorce and Financial Analyst Survey: Certified Divorce Financial Analyst

CDFA®) professionals. (2013) Reveal the Leading Causes of Divorce Retrieved from https://institutedfa.com/Leading-Causes-Divorce/

Wesley life. A Spirit for Living. 20 Stats to Know about Hospice Care in the US. (2014)

https://www.wesleylife.org/blog/news/20-stats-to-know-about-hospice-care-in-the-us.aspxhttps://www.nami.org/mhstats#:~:text=19.1%25%20of%20U.S.%20adults%20experienced,represents%201%20in%2025%20adults.

M & L Special Needs Planning. (2005) Statistics: Reasons for Special Needs Financial Life

Plans. Statistics are from the MetLife's survey The Torn Security Blanket: Children with Special Needs and the Planning Gap" and updated with 2011 Torn Security Blanket Study Retrieved from https://specialneedsplanning.net/statistics/

NAMI, Mental Health by the Numbers, 2020 Nami.org/mhstats

Jennifer Wolf, Verywell Family (2020) U. S. Census Bureau.

Custodial mothers and fathers and their child support: 2015. Updated February 2020.

https://www.verywellfamily.com/single-parent-census-data-2997668

Rebecca Lake, The Balance. How Long do an average marriage last in the U. S? (2020)

Judith Wallerstein, Focus in the Family, (2000) Understanding the impact of divorce. Retrieved from focusonthefamily.ca

National Statistics on Child Abuse, Alliance (2019) et CACs serve far more sexual abuse cases, indicating a deeper problem. https://www.nationalchildrensalliance.org/media-room/national-statistics-on-child-abuse/#:~:text=Nearly%20700%2C000%20children%20are%20abused,kids%20in%20a%20given%20year.

National Center for Educational Statistics, National Bullying Prevention Center, Pacers. (2019)

Bullying statistics, rate of incidences, https://www.pacer.org/bullying/na/stats.asp

Batya Swift Yasgur, MA, LSW, Psychiatry Advisor, 2018 Those Left Behind: Working With Suicide-Bereaved Families Retrieved from psyschiatryadvosor.com